A POCKET FULL OF STONES

WARREN TAYLOR

50 YEARS OF MINISTRY

Story Path

A POCKET FULL OF STONES
WARREN TAYLOR
Copyright © 2024
All rights reserved.
Cover: Georgi James
Image creation: Gencraft.
© 2024 Story Path Publishing.
ISBN: 978-0-6486456-0-3

DEDICATION

I dedicate this book to my precious wife, Annette. Without your believing in me, Honey, I would never have finished it.

ABOUT THE AUTHOR

It is a wonderful privilege and honour for us to share our journey with Warren Taylor for over forty years, which began in the late nineteen seventies and early eighties in the Western Districts of NSW, Australia. We were pioneering a church in the city of Bathurst, NSW, while Warren was pastoring in Dubbo, NSW. Over the years, we have formed a lasting bond of friendship and fellowship.

In Warren, we have recognised his strength in pastoring as that of a true father to the "flock" and the wider Body of Christ, the Church. He is a proven minister of the Gospel, both in word and character. While many have fallen into sin or have been broken in life and ministry, Warren has stood firm in his faith and has faced all the challenges thrown his way.

Over the years, he has reached out many times to those mentioned above in a restorative manner, driven by a compassionate heart to ensure that no one is left behind by the wayside. Warren is Kingdom-minded in his thinking and practice, functioning in the Prophetic/Apostolic role, and is recognised by those who have sat under his ministry. His wisdom has been and still is a blessing to many.

In his book, "Pocket Full of Stones," you will find gemstones that will bless you on your journey through life.

Friends in the journey,
Pastors Peter and Val Mitchison.

ACKNOWLEDGEMENTS

I want to honour our Dear friend of many years, Georgi James, who spent many hours mentoring me in the process of writing this book. An endeavour I had never considered possible. Thank you, Georgi, for your perseverance and patience.

FOREWARD

Warren Taylor's early years in New Zealand shaped a life that would become defined by over 50 years of ministry. As a young teenager, he felt like he didn't fit in, so he sought solace by working on a farm in the picturesque New Zealand countryside. It was here, amidst the natural beauty of the land, that Warren's life took a significant turn. Seated on a fallen tree, he was enveloped by God's loving presence, a moment that marked the beginning of his spiritual voyage and a significant transformation in his life. This encounter was the first of many that paved the way for a life marked by unwavering faith and purpose.

Warren's path to salvation was guided through a series of events that revealed the way to Jesus Christ. Over time, he felt God's presence more strongly, and the doors to Bible college opened for him and his family, a surprising turn of events, especially since he had left school early in life. Despite the challenge of supporting their family with three young children, they found themselves thrust into a journey of faith and obedience, clearly led by God. After Bible College, they embarked on a journey to the Pacific Islands, where they witnessed the miraculous power of God firsthand in their lives. Following this, an opportunity arose for them to go to the notorious Kings Cross area of Sydney, Australia, where they ministered to those struggling with addictions.

At the age of 38, Warren responded to God's call to become the Pastor of his first church in Dubbo, a town in Central Western New South Wales, Australia, known for its wheat farming. Warren and Yvonne dedicated their lives to serving the local church and its community. When the congregation outgrew their small white church building, Warren proposed a bold step by encouraging the church to sell, and purchase land outside of town to build a new church.

Some considered it unusual to choose land so far from the Town Centre, but Warren visualised a church surrounded by homes. His foresight proved remarkable when the city council later developed that area for residential use. Warren, alongside Pastor Arden Burrell from a neighbouring town, who brought engineering skills from farming, embarked on a mission to build a church for 400 people. With the support of a dedicated church community and through many collaborative efforts, they turned this vision into reality. Today, that church stands at the heart of the expanding city. Warren then accepted the role of district overseer, ministering to pastors and leaders.

After pastoring in Dubbo, Warren led other congregations and embarked on extensive international travels, sharing the message of faith and God's transformative love. As a result of Warren's commitment, many individuals were inspired to become full-time ministers and leaders, serving not only within churches but also in various sectors of ministry and business. Warren certainly possesses a remarkable gift for nurturing people's giftings.

Sadly, life took an unexpected turn when Warren's beloved wife, Yvonne, passed away, leaving him overwhelmed with grief. However, his faith in God's promises sustained him and eventually led him to renewed hope and service. During this period, he sought healing and restoration in God's presence.

A few years later, God brought Annette into his life—a woman exemplifying godliness, grace, and inner beauty. After several years of marriage and ministry in Dubbo, they were invited to Pastor the Assembly of God church in Mudgee, where they served for over six years before returning to Dubbo. Together, they continue to minister to people, sharing the ministry of Jesus and the touch of the Holy Spirit. Their partnership is a testament to God's faithfulness and the restoration that can spring forth from deep faith and trust in His divine plan.

Warren's story demonstrates unwavering belief in God's promises, even in the face of adversity, and the transformative power of faith.

As you turn the pages of this book, you will witness the incredible capacity of faith to overcome obstacles and transform lives. Warren's story is a reminder that no matter where we are on our path, God's plan is always greater than our own, and His faithfulness sustains us through every challenge and triumph.

CONTENTS

Chapter 1	The Eye of Faith	15
Chapter 2	Another Good Day in the Kingdom	35
Chapter 3	Living in the Supernatural	49
Chapter 4	Knowing Our Authority	68
Chapter 5	Remaining Connected	77
Chapter 6	Recognising Our Authority	93
Chapter 7	Embracing Divine Power	106
Chapter 8	Anchoring Our Faith	116

Chapter one

THE EYE OF FAITH

As a young lad living in what was a remote part of the South Island of New Zealand, I had no friends that I could hang out with, so I turned to my imagination and discovered that it was an exciting way to pass the time!

There was a single very tall pine tree growing in the neighbour's swamp not far from our house and I discovered that right up at the very top of that tree was a place that I could lay down on my back and drift off into dream land for hours, swaying in the wind and playing out all sorts of scenarios until the shouts of my parents penetrated into my world. I didn't know about faith or about Jesus back then, but looking back, I realised that He knew about me and that more than once, he had saved my life.

The title of this book came from boyhood memories of times of skimming stones on Lake Rotoiti and dreaming about exciting things. As I grew older and left school, I got work on a sheep and cattle property. I absolutely loved the place and the folk that I worked for, but I was still a dreamer! Our heavenly Father loves dreamers! Yes, He really does! You see dreamers become visionaries. Dreamers become good soil for the faith seeds that the Father scatters about. As you read through these pages, my desire is that you catch the "spirit" of the book. Maybe even pick up a flat stone or two and skim them on the waters of faith, allowing your heart to open, and dream once more. I pray that you will encounter the lover of your soul, embracing Him with total surrender.

"In the beginning God created the heavens and the earth." Gen 1:1

In the Hebrew-Greek Key Study Bible, editor Spiros Zodhiates writes: "God, of His own free will and by His absolute power, called the whole universe into being, evoking into existence what was previously non-existent."

So at the beginning of this age, at the very inception of all that exists on this earth, there was a void. The earth was enveloped in darkness, for there was no sun, moon, or stars to illuminate.

In these initial moments, one can imagine a profound sense of God's magnificence and His mighty presence, energy, and power. If we were present at that time, the overwhelming grandeur and divine force shaping the early stages of creation would likely have left an indelible impression on our senses. How
wonderful that would have been there to be a witness to it all. However, it also prompts us to appreciate the present and consider the events unfolding in our own time.
At first glance, this might appear astonishing, but not beyond belief. I could compare it to saying, "At the start of our marriage, I constructed a house." Now that would indeed be astonishing, as I couldn't even lay the foundation by myself! But consider what God accomplished! Out of absolute nothingness, He formed the skies above and the earth beneath, simply by speaking.
"Then God said, "Let there be light": and there was light." Genesis 1:3.
This book doesn't focus on the act of creation itself but, rather, on the potent force of the faith of God that He employed to shape this magnificent world. I firmly believe that everything God says and does is grounded in faith and executed with faith, because He is the very source of faith.

What's even more astonishing is that, as believers, we inherit His divine DNA from the moment we become a new creation! This concept is incredibly significant. Think of it as akin to how we inherit certain traits and characteristics from our earthly parents, only on a spiritual level. Now, let's recall what God said at the beginning of creation.

"Then God said, 'Let Us make man in Our image, according to Our likeness; let them have dominion over the fish of the sea, over the birds of the air, and over the cattle, over all the earth and over every creeping thing that creeps on the earth.' So, God created man in His own image; in the image of God, He created him; male and female He created them." Genesis 1:26-27

I've discovered some great books that discuss faith and offer valuable insights. My writing is inspired by the scripture in Hebrews 11:13. This verse describes the faithful as those who passed away without the fulfilment of God's promises yet still believed. They saw and greeted these promises from afar, acknowledging themselves as foreigners and pilgrims on the earth. "But without faith it is impossible to please Him, for he who comes to God must believe that He is, and that He is a rewarder of those who diligently seek Him." Hebrews 11:6.

This verse hits home for me because it's all about having faith in promises that we might not see fulfilled in our lifetime. It's about believing in something, even when it's not right in front of us. Believing because God has spoken it to us, perhaps through a prophetic word or a revelation from a passage in scripture.

Jesus taught simple, powerful lessons about overcoming wrong with truth, justice, kindness, and mercy. They're straightforward but also make you think. He came to destroy evil and sin with truth, righteousness, love, and forgiveness.

"He who sins is of the devil, for the devil has sinned from the beginning. For this purpose, the Son of God was manifested, that He might destroy the works of the devil." 1 John 3:8

In simple terms, Jesus gave us the choice to live a good, virtuous, and exciting life, and not to get caught up in wrong things. His teachings encourage us to think about the choices we make on our journey through life.

My mind goes to a young man whom I will call Bob. He was full of zeal for Jesus and determined to spread the gospel to places where it had never been preached. Bob, along with his wife, fearlessly trekked through dense jungles and waded through rivers, driven by an all-consuming love for God that burned within their hearts. Miracles happened through their ministry, people were healed, and souls were saved. It was an exhilarating yet exhausting phase of their journey with God.

Then, one day, Bob noticed a small lump in his ear that felt tender. He consulted a doctor to determine its nature. The lump turned out to be skin cancer, a condition that could have been readily treated. However, what followed tragically cost him his life. Bob firmly believed that God would heal him and rejected all medical help. Unfortunately, this decision allowed the cancer to advance into his head.

This serves as a vital lesson: we must not live by presumption. As a faith people, our faith is not only rooted in the written word of God but also in hearing and understanding the "now" revelatory Word of God to us. Bob's error lay in presuming that God would heal him without receiving clear guidance from God Himself. While it may appear stern, God's love for us mirrors the love of a true Father.

Bob had a deep understanding of the scriptures, believing that nothing was impossible for God. He expected to experience healing as a powerful testimony of God's love and omnipotence. However, it's important to remember that we cannot manipulate God or coerce Him into acting according to our desires (imagine trying to do that!). At times, we all make wrong choices, but the remarkable thing is that God's love remains unwavering.

Here's an interesting fact: our Heavenly Father doesn't dwell on our past; instead, He focuses on our present and future. He accepts every moment of our journey with love and grace. It's a beautiful reminder that God is indeed a God of restoration.

As I explore faith and Jesus' teachings, I want to dig deeper into how faith, hope, and our choices can transform our lives for the better. I believe this is important, and I pray these pages will inspire and guide you to understand and adhere to the teachings of Jesus Christ for a fuller and richer life. Kingdom living is the most exciting way to live! It challenges and shakes off the shackles of the religious spirit that seeks to blind our eyes and deafen our ears! When the disciples asked Jesus to teach them how to pray, Jesus responded with a groundbreaking teaching that would have amazed the disciples. Matthew 6:9-13.

"In this manner, therefore, pray: Our Father in heaven, Hallowed be Your name. Your kingdom come. Your will be done on earth as it is in heaven. Give us this day our daily bread. And forgive us our debts, As we forgive our debtors. And do not lead us into temptation. But deliver us from the evil one. For Yours is the kingdom and the power and the glory forever. Amen."

My own experience of salvation was an occurrence orchestrated by the Holy Spirit. It transpired in 1968 after sustaining a back injury while working on a farm along the Kaikoura Coast in New Zealand's South Island. After multiple unsuccessful attempts to heal the injury, my mother suggested I visit a chiropractor in Nelson. It was an era when these practitioners were often seen as quacks or charlatans.

I headed to Nelson and dropped by my parent's place for a visit before my appointment. At that point, the Holy Spirit took the reins. A man arrived at the door, coincidentally the minister of the Anglican Church my parents attended. This man, named Peter, was a Spirit-filled servant of God who had previously served as a Naval Chaplain, making him adept at dealing with stubborn individuals like me.

During our conversation (In which my parents mysteriously vanished), I noticed another presence in the room. I voiced this to the minister, who responded with joy, affirming that Jesus was indeed present, and left it at that.

This marked the beginning of a profound shift in my life, as well as in the lives of my wife Yvonne (now in glory, experiencing the riches of heaven) and our three children Shane, Ian, and Michelle. I never made it to the chiropractor, as I missed the appointment. My back troubles persisted, leading us to leave farming and move to town. Unbeknownst to me, this was part of God's plan.

"The steps of a good man are ordered by the Lord, And He delights in his way." Psalm 37:23

Shortly after settling into our new home and my job as an assistant greenkeeper at the local golf course, we came across two ministers—one of whom was the pastor of the Elim Pentecostal Church in Stoke. These men shared the Gospel of Jesus Christ with us, and I discovered that feeling or sensing God's presence was one thing but experiencing the formidable power of the Holy Spirit required repentance from sin, acceptance of Jesus Christ as my Lord and Saviour, and being born again in spirit. This marked the true beginning of our journey of faith!

Those days of the sixties and seventies were the foundation of our walking with the glory of God upon us, together with signs and wonders that we both witnessed and were a part of.

These were the days of the charismatic outpouring that came to New Zealand in the 1960s, a move of the Holy Spirit that brought Anglican, Catholic, Pentecostal, and Evangelical churches together. During one of the conferences, I watched as Catholic Nuns danced before the Lord with Anglican and Pentecostal Ministers on the stage. Surely this had to be God! People got up and testified about being healed and others about being delivered from evil spirits. And I want to tell you I thought that must be what church life was like! Was I in for a shock? Sunday service was "the same old, same old" – lovely people, a great Pastor, but they were deaf to what the Holy Spirit was saying and bringing to us.

It was during this time of outpouring that our church had a visiting speaker, Pastor Des Short, and what a preacher he was! I hung onto every word and let it soak into my spirit. On the last night after the meeting was over, when we were putting away chairs, I walked past my Pastor who was talking to Pastor Short. He reached out and grabbed my arm, saying to Des, "You need more students like this man to come to your college." Well, I got myself free and fled! The word 'college' was just NOT in my vocabulary at that time! However, I could not get it out of my mind, so my late wife Yvonne and I prayed about it and God spoke clearly to us both that we were to go and, as it turned out, that was a divine encounter and an invitation to learn to walk in faith in the financial realm as we had no savings and it was a full-time, short-term College, AND it was called Faith Bible College. It was worth every bit of sacrifice that I would do again, to watch how my Father God met every financial need and caused our old Standard Vanguard car to run on an empty tank for days until some money appeared.

This was not an unusual miracle in those days. I remember a Tongan Missionary teaching us in college about faith and his testimony about the time when he was in Papua New Guinea working with Youth With A Mission. They had arrived in a remote village up in the hills and had stopped to talk with some folk there, on getting back to their car, he noticed that the fuel light was on saying the tank was empty. They were nowhere near a fuel station, plus the fact that no one in the team had any money. So, they prayed (that's what you do when all else fails!) As they were all worshipping and praising God, Kolafi was watching the fuel gauge, and, to his joy, he saw the needle beginning to rise and it went to full! He said, "I jumped out of the car and went and took the cap off the tank, and saw the petrol was almost running out of the top! This was an enormous boost for us College students as we had to do weekend ministry trips taking no money with us, as part of our training.

Divine encounters have been a part of our lives for many years now, but they are always exciting, whether great or small and sometimes we do not recognise them until later on while talking things over.

During that era, a mighty spiritual renewal movement swept through New Zealand, characterised by the demonstration of the power of the Holy Spirit. We witnessed and took part in countless extraordinary healings, demonic deliverances, and miracles. Leg lengthening was one of the miracles that was unusual at that time. It was when someone was born with one leg shorter than the other, or through some disease that had affected that area. Just to witness the leg growing was amazing, but to be the one praying and to feel the leg getting longer was an unforgettable experience. After some time, we considered the manifestation of the Holy Spirit to be the norm in "church." This powerful presence and anointing persisted into the early 1980s.

This move of God was not just an isolated event. When God led us to Australia in December 1974, we had been in Tonga working with the Youth With A Mission team. We could only get a three-month renewable visa when we arrived, and at the end of those months, we felt our time there had finished. We were praying for God's leading, and the mail arrived with a letter from a fellow Faith Bible College student asking us to pray about going to Australia to work with Teen Challenge. Both Yvonne and I had a genuine sense that this was from God, and so, off we went to new adventures of the Heavenly nature!

In Australia, the Holy Spirit's presence swept through the Nation, an extraordinary move that continued well into the 1980s before gradually waning. While several factors might explain this decline, one fundamental truth remains, God's unwavering desire for His people to be reached. Unfortunately, at times, individuals have attempted to control and claim ownership of the Holy Spirit's work within the church, often without a complete understanding of the person and power of the Holy Spirit.

I often ponder a crucial question: Will Jesus find people with 'unwavering faith' when He returns to Earth? This question is explored in Luke 18:1-8, where Jesus tells a parable. In it, He points out how important it is to pray persistently and have faith that doesn't waver. In his message, he emphasizes the significance of praying persistently and maintaining an unwavering faith in all circumstances. He highlights that prayer is not merely a onetime act, but a continuous and consistent conversation with Yahweh. Through persistent prayer, we can strengthen our connection with God and find solace, guidance, and support. Additionally, he emphasises that a faith that doesn't waver, even in the face of challenges or doubts, is essential for spiritual growth and resilience. Such unwavering faith allows individuals to trust in the divine plan, knowing that everything happens for a reason and that their prayers will be answered in the most appropriate way and time. Overall, his message encourages believers to cultivate a persistent prayer life and to hold on to an unshakeable faith, recognising the transformative power of these practices in their spiritual journey.

Luke 18:1 Then He spoke a parable to them, that men always ought to pray and not lose heart, [2] saying: "There was in a certain city a judge who did not fear God nor regard man. [3] Now there was a widow in that city, and she came to him, saying, 'Get justice for me from my adversary.' [4] And he would not for a while; but afterward he said within himself. Though I do not fear God nor regard man, [5] yet because this widow troubles me I will avenge her, lest by her continual coming she weary me." [6]

Then the Lord said, "Hear what the unjust judge said. ⁷ And shall God not avenge His own elect who cry out day and night to Him, though He bears long with them? ⁸ I tell you that He will avenge them speedily. Nevertheless, when the Son of Man comes, will He really find faith on the earth?"

The parable revolves around a judge who doesn't fear God or care much about people, and a persistent widow who continually keeps asking him for help. Eventually, the judge gives in because of her unrelenting requests. Jesus uses this story to teach us that if even an unjust judge responds to persistence, then surely God who is fair and compassionate, will answer the persistent prayers of His chosen ones. Jesus ends with a powerful question:

It becomes clear that what truly pleases God isn't our achievements, but the faith we have. The people mentioned in Hebrews chapter 11, lived their lives with a focus on God's ultimate plan, seeing it through the lens of faith.

"Now faith is the substance of things hoped for, the evidence of things not seen." Hebrews 11:1

They saw themselves as wanderers and outsiders in this world, relying on faith as their compass. These folks pleased God by trusting in Him and acknowledging His existence. Trusting in God is absolutely crucial. Romans 12:3 underscores this by stating that each person is given a measure of faith through God's grace.

Reflecting on my journey of faith, I see how the Holy Spirit was my guide and teacher in those formative years. I find myself thankful for His divine guidance, as it meant that we were not merely indoctrinated into rigid 'church' doctrine but were led to understand the more fluid and profound ways of the Holy Spirit. This was a blessing, as human mentors did not shape our path, allowing us to follow a course directed by spiritual insights. Since being baptised in the Holy Spirit and beginning to speak in tongues, my experience has been enriched with spiritual gifts, like receiving words of knowledge, discerning spirits, prophesying, witnessing healings, and exercising authority over demonic forces. These profound experiences have been integral to my faith journey. This was walking in faith for me, as I've always felt blessed by God's goodness, and that feeling continues today because He never changes, and His mercy is everlasting. This life is for all who believe in Him. It's not just for the favoured few, as there is no such thing!

About a year after being baptised, I had a supernatural encounter. I was asleep when a loud voice woke me up by calling my name. Instantly awake, I responded, "Yes, Lord" This event occurred over five decades ago, yet its clarity remains undiminished. My faith in God has remained unwavering since then.

It's truly remarkable to be called by God Himself, to hear His voice with such clarity, especially when I was far from perfect. Now, you might wonder if He would do the same for you. The answer is a resounding yes! He loves you passionately, and if calling your name is what's best for you, then He will undoubtedly do so. However, God might have a unique way to touch your heart, one that's different from what worked for me. So, reflect on His love for you, rather than on what He can achieve through you. Remember, God cherishes and loves His children; He doesn't use or oppress them.

To me, faith is like a bedrock, a firm foundation that supports us as we venture into the realm of the supernatural in our own lives and the lives of those around us. It's the sturdy bridge that allows us to access the divine.

"The steps of a good man are ordered by the Lord, and He delights in his way."

This verse reminds us that God not only guides our steps but also takes pleasure in the journey we undertake with Him. It's an invitation to walk confidently, knowing that God is with us every step of the way.

In my experience, it often seems that our Heavenly Father desires us to revel in the journey itself. Unfortunately, we can sometimes get entangled in complex theological debates, conflicting doctrines, and the overwhelming burdens of the world. These distractions can lead us to lose sight of the profound beauty, unconditional love, and unreserved acceptance offered by Yahweh.

Allow me to share a remarkable encounter from my time at an Anglican Church in Darlinghurst, Sydney. A young man walked into my office after years of searching for spiritual truth. He had explored the teachings of various gurus and embarked on a spiritual journey across the East, but it all proved fruitless.

As we talked, I shared the Gospel of Jesus Christ with him. During our conversation, he became increasingly uneasy, and it even escalated to manifestations of demonic influence. However, I addressed these issues as he renounced the gods associated with the cults he had encountered during his quest. He willingly surrendered his heart to Jesus, and the transformation was extraordinary. He became a "new creation," and there was even a visible change in the colour of his eyes. It was a moment of profound joy, as if the heavens themselves were celebrating his newfound faith.

"So then faith comes by hearing, and hearing by the word of God." Romans 10:17

This verse highlights the importance of revelation. The Greek word for "hearing" here, "akoe," goes beyond just listening; it suggests that hearing with our hearts can transport us to a higher dimension of understanding. Revelation, derived from the Scriptures, has the power to transport us into communion with the living God, bringing about a transformation within us. We are continually changed, growing from one level of glory to another through revelation.

I cannot emphasise enough the importance of reading the scriptures regularly and meditating on those parts that seem to light up or jump off the page at you because this is where we get revelation coming from the Holy Spirit, who is our Teacher.

When the devil was tempting Jesus in the wilderness, he challenged Him to change stones into bread, but Jesus calmly responded. "It is written, 'Man shall not live by bread alone, but by every word that proceeds from the mouth of God'" Matthew 4:4

In John 16:15a, Jesus speaks of the Holy Spirit, saying, 'He will take of what is Mine and declare it to you.' This means that we are a people privileged to receive unveiled truths through revelation. As we step out in faith, guided by the insights we gain, we do so with a sense of knowing something new, vibrant, and filled with life.

Faith is not just a concept but a sturdy foundation and a reliable bridge that supports us as we reach out for the supernatural, both in our own lives and in the lives of others. It's an integral part of our journey, helping us navigate the wonder of a life in union and oneness with Jesus.

It's hard to keep your feet on the ground when you begin to 'see' what the Holy Spirit is taking us into in these days that lay ahead. Just imagine what it could look like if the Spirit of Might came upon you when you were in the midst of people in great suffering and distress! Woo Hoo! That would knock the stuffing out of dry, dead religion!

Chapter two

ANOTHER GOOD DAY IN THE KINGDOM

I have named this chapter "Another Good Day in the Kingdom" because I believe that every day is a good day in Yahweh's Kingdom!

It's intriguing to observe that Jesus never fixated on the challenges His disciples undoubtedly faced in their lives. Instead, He straightforwardly taught them how to achieve victory, how to overcome, and what to expect by following Him. Annette and I have engaged in many years of pastoral counselling, and through this, we discovered that the most significant deficiency in people's lives was a lack of awareness about their identity and their position in Christ.

My start in life was, I guess, like many others who were born through the years of the Second World War. Whilst my Mum was in hospital having nearly died bringing me into the world, I was put into the care of an older couple because my dad was in the New Zealand Home Guard and also working.

During my early years, spanning from childhood to my twenties, I grappled with feelings of inferiority and rejection. The impact was so profound that I struggled to establish friendships and often felt unwanted. At fifteen, I left school and started working in a remote region of New Zealand. This suited me well. I found enjoyment in the demanding work, and the boss and his wife treated me kindly. I learned to shoot wild pigs that posed a threat to newborn lambs during lambing, and I also honed my skills in hunting deer and fishing. However, my educational pursuits had to take a backseat. I spent a few years working in that area before deciding to join the Air Force and get an apprenticeship as a motor mechanic. However, when I signed up, they told me that there weren't any vacancies for motor mechanics and put me in as a driver.

Well, I got so bored just polishing trucks and keeping out of sight that I took the option of getting out within the first three months and went back to see if I could get my old job back. Sadly, all I could get was a week of fencing.

It was during this time that I had my second experience with Jesus. It was while I was out deer stalking that I had a profound visitation that went beyond anything that I had experienced of the "mystical" kind. As I walked through the quiet native bush, I sat down on a fallen tree. At that moment, an intense silence surrounded me. It was far more intense than my first experience, and I felt an overwhelming sense of awe. At the time, I couldn't fully comprehend what was happening, but looking back, I now recognise it as the first touch of a loving and wonderful God in my life.

If you feel close to the Holy Spirit while reading this, stop for a bit. Close your eyes, take a deep breath, and feel God's presence with you. God isn't far away; He's here with us, just like He was in the upper room in Acts chapter two. You can experience God's presence right where you are. In the stillness of your innermost being, silently seek for God to make Himself known to you. Ask Him to speak to you, whether through a gentle impression, a thought, or a scripture verse. Be receptive to His guidance. While going about your daily activities, be mindful of His presence and be receptive to any promptings you may receive. By simply listening and seeking His presence, you can take your first practical step towards developing a deeper relationship with God.

'Call to Me, and I will answer you, and show you great and mighty things, which you do not know.' Jeremiah 33:3 NKJV

His presence carries power, and wherever He is, His power manifests. That's just how He operates! The day the Holy Spirit descended upon those gathered in the upper room in Jerusalem, an ancient prophecy spoken by the prophet Joel was fulfilled in Acts 2:1-4.

[1] "When the Day of Pentecost had fully come, they were all with one accord in one place. [2] And suddenly there came a sound from heaven, as of a rushing mighty wind, and it filled the whole house where they were sitting. [3] Then there appeared to them divided tongues, as of fire, and one sat upon each of them. [4] And they were all filled with the Holy Spirit and began to speak with other tongues, as the Spirit gave them utterance."

Joel 2:28-29 says, "And it shall come to pass afterward that I will pour out My Spirit on all flesh; Your sons and your daughters shall prophesy, your old men shall dream dreams, Your young men shall see visions. And also, on My menservants and My maidservants, I will pour out My Spirit in those days."

By the use of the terminology "I will pour out My Spirit in those days," it is clear that Joel's prophecy wasn't a onetime event. Instead, it was a prophecy meant for the era we currently live in and the one into which we were born. The original intention of his words, when he first uttered them, was for the present moment. Hallelujah!

Why is God's presence seemingly less apparent in today's world? It could be because the Church has strayed from simply trusting in who 'He IS.'

Some individuals recall the mighty acts of God in the past but may overlook His ongoing power in the present. The unchanging nature of God enables us to experience His presence and power through faith in the current moment.

How can a church lacking in power become a formidable adversary to the enemy of our souls? Could a revival be the answer? Although attempted before, its effectiveness was limited to a certain period, as people eventually grew tired, resulting in a decline in impact.

I know of one church in our area that is doing great, and it is because of their hearts after God and the fact that they have determined to let the Holy Spirit run every meeting. They don't take up offerings or talk about tithing and yet they are one of the top givers in their movement and their meetings are filled with the presence of God and the power of the Holy Spirit. Folk get healed, saved, and filled with the Spirit. I so loved it when I preached there. They were so desirous to hear the word of God that they almost drew it out of me, and hey, they were really happy people! Now there's a thing!

"I will pour out my Spirit on all flesh" signifies God's intention to make His Spirit accessible to people of every background. The Holy Spirit is available to all who believe in Jesus Christ.

"Your sons and your daughters shall prophesy": Both men and women will be empowered to speak forth God's word, highlighting the inclusiveness of spiritual gifts.

"Your old men shall dream dreams, your young men shall see visions": God's Spirit will inspire individuals of all ages, providing revelation through dreams and visions.

"Even on the male and female servants in those days I will pour out my Spirit": This emphasizes the indiscriminate nature of the outpouring, reaching the humblest members of society.

Overall, Joel's prophecy anticipates a time when God's Spirit will empower and inspire people from all walks of life, emphasising Yahweh's desire to communicate with all people, everywhere.

I had the privilege of witnessing a remarkable event. For three hours, I observed God's power flow into a young woman who had been suffering from a degenerative spinal condition because of an accident. She had been enduring excruciating pain, requiring frequent hospital injections, and her medical prognosis had foreseen her in a wheelchair within six months. However, something incredible happened. She experienced a radical and complete healing. As God's power surged through her, she exclaimed, "I can feel my hands warming up" and "my feet are tingling and hot." With this newfound strength and flexibility, she was able to return to her work as a Naval photographer. This serves as a powerful testament to the God we worship—a God filled with compassion, mercy, and love. He never turns away from those who approach Him with humility and contrition.

"Let not your heart be troubled; you believe in God, believe also in Me." John 14:1.

In this passage, Jesus addresses His disciples before His crucifixion. Despite having spent three years with Him, they still required reassurance of their faith in Him. How could this be? They had witnessed His miracles and teachings and even been empowered by Him to preach and heal. Yet, they hadn't fully known Him—His heart and His ways.

I urge you to set aside this book momentarily and pick up the Bible. Read through chapters 14, 15, and 16 of the Gospel of John. Meditate until you sense not only God's love and presence but also hear His voice in your heart. Jesus promised in John 16:13: "However, when He, the Spirit of truth, has come, He will guide you into all truth; for He will not speak on His own authority, but whatever He hears He will speak, and He will tell you things to come." John 16:13.

The Holy Spirit, known as the Spirit of truth, will lead believers into understanding all truth and reveal future events. In our current times, we shouldn't blindly follow every word from a prophet or a preacher. Instead, every believer needs to learn to listen to God's voice directly. We are part of the Bride that Jesus will return for, so we must know the present day. We should make the most of each day by worshipping, reading the scriptures, and reflecting on passages that describe our transformation into sons of God and our destiny in Him.

Some of my favourite scriptures are Acts 17:28, 1 Corinthians 6:17, Galatians 2:20, and 1 John 4:17. I like to personalise these verses, making them feel like God is speaking directly to me. Try meditating on these yourself and don't stop until you feel and sense the Holy Spirit coming on you in might and power!

"But the Helper, the Holy Spirit, whom the Father will send in My name, He will teach you all things and bring to your remembrance all things that I said to you." John 14:26

I remember when, as a young Pastor with my first church, I got up early in the morning each day and went off to the church building where I would pray in tongues for an hour and then in my understanding for an hour, I would then speed read one-seventh of the bible, and then meditatively read it for the next hour. I did this six days a week, right up until we started building the new church structure. During this time, I was invited to teach at a Bible College in Sydney. After I had finished my first day, some of the students came up to me asking how I learned the scriptures so well that I could link the Old Testament and New Testament without looking them up. It was because my early morning discipline had created a well of life within me that the Holy Spirit brought back to me, and I just overflowed!

The Holy Spirit will glorify Jesus and reveal His teachings. This intimacy is the Father's desire, that we become His sons and daughters, knowing Him deeply, rather than mere servants following commands.

You, too, can do that. If you have given your life to Jesus Christ, then you are a son or daughter of God and are immersed in Him.

The message conveyed in 1 John 3:1-3 is both powerful and touching. It speaks to the boundless nature of God's love, which designates us as His children. This concept beautifully captures the fact that we are currently embraced as God's children, enveloped in His affection and care.

Delving deeper into this idea, we find that this passage also hints at something transformative on the horizon. While the precise details of our future selves remain uncertain, it assures us that an incredible change awaits. When Christ returns, this transformation will take place, bringing us more completely into His likeness.

"Behold what manner of love the Father has bestowed on us, that we should be called children of God! Therefore, the world does not know us, because it did not know Him. Beloved, now we are children of God; and it has not yet been revealed what we shall be, but we know that when He is revealed, we shall be like Him, for we shall see Him as He is. And everyone who has this hope in Him purifies himself, just as He is pure." 1 John 3:1-3.

This process of transformation is linked with hope, a hope that motivates us to strive for purity, mirroring the purity of Christ. It's akin to looking forward to an exciting event, a step towards becoming who we are truly meant to be.

My testimony, while not being so dramatic as some, is an example of the all-encompassing power of His love towards us. Remember, God does not look at our past, only the present and the future; the past was dealt with at the cross where Jesus took us into His death and then raised us with Him in His resurrection. So, we can state joyfully:

"My old identity has been co-crucified with Messiah and no longer lives; for the Anointed One lives His life through me, we live in union as one! My new life is empowered by the faith of the Son of God who loves me so much that he gave Himself for me and dispenses His life into mine.'" (Galatians 2:20 TPT).

When I gave my heart to Jesus, He took it and did amazing things to it. At the time of this happening, I was employed as a shepherd/farmhand. My dogs had only seen and heard the old me. The first time I went to muster the sheep, my dogs just stood and stared! I no longer swore at them! I no longer threatened them with a fate worse than death if they disobeyed an order or direction! I laugh about it now, but I had to learn a whole new way of working and speaking to them that conveyed authority and dominion.

Ultimately, when Christ makes His appearance, everything will change. We will experience a transformation – not into something extraordinary, but into individuals transformed into the image of Jesus, which leaves even extraordinary for dead!

It's akin to gaining access to the inner circle and understanding who Jesus truly is. Essentially, 1 John 3:2 says that we are presently embraced as God's children.

"Beloved, now we are children of God; and it has not yet been revealed what we shall be, but we know that when He is revealed, we shall be like Him, for we shall see Him as He is."

Although the detail of our future transformation remains undisclosed, we can hold on to the assurance that, with Christ's return, we will be fully transformed into His likeness. This verse emphasises themes of hope and transformation, highlighting the deep connection between believers and Christ as they journey toward becoming more like Him.

A poignant moment in my life during a Bible College outreach comes to mind. I was part of a team leading the Sunday morning service in a small village in New Zealand. As we worshipped, the leader sang the chorus, "Jesus is alive." This simple song struck me profoundly.

Yes, Jesus was alive, and He was alive in me! Now an extrovert, I am not! However, this realisation transformed my mindset from one of a servant to that of a son, and I just could not stop dancing and shouting in the aisle between the seats!

It was a revelation that ushered me into acceptance and intimacy with my Heavenly Father. To this day, His presence and love mean more to me than all the miracles and gifts I have had the privilege to experience.

I appreciate Bill Johnson's book title, "Hosting God," as it encapsulates the essence of our relationship with God. Just as I discovered Jesus alive within me, we have the incredible opportunity to host His presence and experience His deeply personal love moment by moment.

Hosting God is all about being aware of His Presence in you, every step, every moment. It is walking in the reverential fear of God at all times. Being aware of our thoughts, our words, and our attitude toward others and ourselves. Guarding at all times the eye gate, what you allow in and through your ear gate, what you allow yourself to listen to. I use "allow" to really stress how important this is. What you carry in the spirit is more precious than all the wealth in the world! And it is a free gift. Our part is to treasure the One within and keep our hearts pure and our love strong for Him.

Chapter three

LIVING IN THE SUPERNATURAL

I am fully persuaded that living and walking in the supernatural realms of the Kingdom is the very essence of God's intention for us, both in the present moment and always. I aspire to achieve an increasingly supernatural way of life constantly. Jesus instructed us to pray for the immediate arrival of His Kingdom and for God's will to be executed on earth just as it is in Heaven and because Yahweh is naturally supernatural, everything He involves Himself in carries that supernatural quality. He takes great delight in observing our exploration of this realm as we carry His very nature and have His DNA.

The supernatural has always been a captivating aspect of human spirituality, and the Bible provides a rich tapestry of stories and teachings that delve into this mysterious realm. In the pages of scripture, we find divine encounters, miracles, and unexplainable phenomena that remind us of the extraordinary power and presence of Yahweh. Join me now on a journey to explore the nature of the supernatural as revealed in the Word of God.

When discussing this topic, many people often turn to the gifts of the Holy Spirit described in 1 Corinthians 12:4-11. However, it's important to recognise that these gifts are given as the Holy Spirit wills. We never own them. They are holy and precious gifts that flow through us to the ones needing them.

The Revelation Gifts

In my experience, these often happen as a result of our time spent in the quiet place, worshipping, and praising the One who loves us far and above that which we could imagine. Revelation can come suddenly, even when you are reading a novel or watching a movie. But I believe that the deepest revelations come when our entire focus is on the Father. Always remember, that His gifts to us are for all of His children and not just the man or woman behind the pulpit. Usually, the only reason they seem to be so deep is because of the time spent as outlined above in this chapter. It does not depend on your level of schooling or the number of letters after your name. I left school at age 15 and then went to work at the labouring level. I didn't even realise that there was a New Testament and an Old Testament, but the Holy Spirit came alongside me and began to teach me about matters of the spiritual realm, not just the intellectual realm.

Your Father in heaven will go to any lengths to bring you to maturity in the area that He has set out for you. Jeremiah 29:11 "For I know the plans that I have for you, declares the Lord, plans for welfare and not for calamity to give you a future and a hope."

Word of Wisdom: This is the ability to receive and release divine wisdom and insight to specific situations and problems. Wisdom is one of the priority gifts needed in the counselling room. It works well with prophetic insight. Most times wisdom surprises me as I can chat with someone and suddenly my mind is saying, "Where did that come from? That was real wisdom".

Word of Knowledge: This gift involves the supernatural ability to have knowledge or information about a person, event, or circumstance that would not be known through natural means. It's knowledge that comes directly from the Holy Spirit.

Shortly after being baptised in the Holy Spirit, I worked as an assistant greenkeeper at a golf course. Next to our machinery shed was a house that used to be part of the golf club. One day during our coffee break, a young teenager had trouble starting his car after washing it. I suddenly knew exactly what was wrong with it and I mentioned this to my boss who was very disbelieving, but he went out and told the young man what I had said - that if he checked the distributor, he would find the rotor was missing. He followed the instructions and sure enough, there was no rotor. I also had suggested he check the rag he had used to cover the distributor while washing the car, and he found the missing rotor there. His astonishment was evident.

This experience showed me that God can provide specific knowledge, even in non-spiritual situations, to show His care and involvement in every aspect of our lives. It also reveals to us that God is not "religious"; He is not bound by Church doctrines or procedures. He shows us He is the source of freedom.

Discerning of Spirits: This gift allows a person to discern the source of a spiritual manifestation, whether it's from God, a demonic spirit, or human motives. It operates through discernment and faith in the Holy Spirit's guidance.

I remember a time when I was Pastoring an Assembly of God Church in Sydney, Australia when I was asked if I would minister to a young lady who was being harassed by evil spirits. I agreed to pray for her, and we were to meet at an Anglican church, about a 30-minute drive away from us.

We arrived and parked in the car park, and just as I got out of the car, the other folks arrived and parked as far away from us as they could! As I stood up, this lady was getting out of her friend's car, and our eyes met across the parking lot. The moment that happened, she lost control and frantically tried to get back into the car. Why? I hear you ask. Thank you for asking! It was because the evil spirits in her recognized the authority of Jesus Christ in me and knew they were defeated.

We went on into the office that had been opened for us and waited. It only took about ten or fifteen minutes, and she arrived at the door, where my wife met her and ushered her inside. She shared her situation, and we prayed with her, casting out the demons. Then, we asked the Holy Spirit to fill the entire area where the demons had been. As she was still very shaken by all of this, my wife kindly invited her to come home with us for a while. I had to leave for another situation, so Yvonne stayed with her. As they sat together, the woman began to manifest again and attempted to leave. At that moment, my amazing wife asked the Lord to lock the door, and remarkably, He did! So, despite her efforts, she couldn't open the door until I returned, and I didn't even need to use the key. We again ministered to her and sought healing from the Lord for her soul that had been so battered. She finally left free and happy.

The Power gifts

The Gift of Special Faith: This is an amazing gift that I have received on a few occasions. One such occasion was when we left New Zealand to minister in Tonga. In Tonga, I wasn't able to work, as only one out of every ten could secure a job, and we had no support from anywhere. With three young children, we certainly needed that wonderful gift in our lives! We journeyed through the school of faith at a depth that I had thought was not possible to experience. It was a strange country, with an unfamiliar language and no external support. Despite these challenges, we never went without a meal, and we never missed paying the rent, even though there were five of us. God is incredibly faithful and so very good!

This extraordinary gift empowers individuals to possess unwavering faith in situations that seem impossible by human standards. It goes beyond the ordinary faith every believer possesses and allows someone to confidently believe in a supernatural outcome. This gift often emerges in times of crisis, where a person with the gift of special faith can encourage and lead others to trust in God's miraculous intervention. They serve as beacons of hope and catalysts for extraordinary breakthroughs, inspiring the entire congregation to stand firm in their faith.

Gifts of Healing: This is the ability to heal physical, emotional, or spiritual ailments through the power of the Holy Spirit. It operates through prayer and the laying on of hands, and it requires faith in God's healing power.

During our time in Fiji, my late wife, Yvonne, and I visited a tiny village nestled atop a high hill. The hills on this island were lush and covered in abundant vegetation. We made the arduous trek on foot, enduring the humid conditions. Our exertions promptly wiped away any romanticism associated with our endeavour. Eventually, we reached the village and entered a small, low hut. We had to stoop to fit through the doorway.

Inside, the room was dimly lit, with no candles or lamps. The meagre contents included a bed, a fireplace, and a few buckets. Amid this simplicity sat a very elderly woman, purportedly one hundred and ten years old and blind. We were asked to pray for her sight to be restored.

Our purpose in Fiji was to showcase God's power, wonder, and love to these beautiful people. Placing our hands on her head, we offered a simple prayer of faith, entreating the Lord to heal her eyes. When we concluded, Yvonne inquired if she could see. The elderly lady calmly opened her eyes and matter-of-factly announced that she could indeed see. Her daughter, accompanying us, burst into tears of joy. Yvonne further asked, "What colour is my hair?" The woman scrutinised her and replied, "It's neither black nor brown—it's somewhere in between," (Remember it was a very dim hut). Her description was precisely accurate, and we rejoiced with her in celebration and praise to God. In a neighbouring hut, Jesus healed a deaf man, prompting his wife to joyfully exclaim, "Now I won't have to keep shouting at him!"

There is not a hard and fast rule on how God works, as each person is special to Him. While in Fiji, I was asked to pray for a man who had really bad sugar diabetes. I prayed for him as we were leaving to go further inland. On our way back, we had the chance to see how this guy had got on. His wife said the moment I went out the door, he flushed all of his medications down the toilet and has been better ever since! Thank you, Jesus!

Working of Miracles: This gift involves the ability to perform supernatural acts that go beyond the natural laws. It includes events like raising the dead or controlling the elements. It operates through faith in God's ability to intervene supernaturally.

I have yet to see the dead raised or a severed limb replaced. I have heard joints popping back into place and watched physically disabled people walk again, deaf ears opened, and blind eyes seeing again.

Once again, this gift is best received through intimacy with the Father, as knowing Him must be our priority and not the gifts. Power gifts can puff us up if we are not firmly settled in our love for Him.

The Utterance Gifts

Prophecy: Remember, we do not own the gifts or the callings; they always belong to Jesus.

The gift of prophecy does not make one a Prophet, as one is a gift and the other is a calling to the ministry of a Prophet, The Gift is to the body of believers to bring comfort, edification, and exhortation and can reveal the unknown things, bringing them into the light.

Speaking in Tongues: This is the supernatural ability to speak in languages unknown to the speaker, often in a prayer or worship context. It operates through faith in the Holy Spirit's empowerment. A message in tongues during a service or gathering of people must be interpreted; otherwise, it is unfruitful.

Interpretation of Tongues: This gift is the ability to interpret the messages spoken in tongues so that others can understand and benefit from them. It operates through faith and a reliance on the Holy Spirit for understanding.

Faith enables individuals to step out in obedience, believing that the Holy Spirit will work through them to accomplish His purposes. However, it's important to note that interpretations and practices of these gifts can vary among different Christian denominations and traditions.

I share these accounts not only to magnify God but also because "The testimony of Jesus is the spirit of prophecy" (Revelation 19:10b). Our testimonies possess a prophetic quality that can lead listeners into a dynamic encounter with the Saviour. I view testimonies as being on a par with revelation, as they can unlock the place where you are stuck and open up new realms with fresh understanding. If you're open to hearing, you're bound to experience a life-altering encounter with the Living God. The Apostle Paul bluntly captures this concept in:

2 Corinthians 3:7 "But if the ministry of death, written and engraved on stones, was glorious so that the children of Israel could not look steadily at the face of Moses because of the glory of his countenance, which glory was passing away, how will the ministry of the Spirit not be more glorious?"

Imagine the journey of the Hebrew people. Throughout their generation, their laws of faith were etched onto hardened stone tablets. These tablets stood as a symbol of authority, but they also brought a heavy burden. The people living under these rules found themselves ensnared and weighed down.

2 Corinthians 3:17-18 "Now the Lord is the Spirit, and where the Spirit of the Lord is, there is liberty. But we all, with unveiled face, beholding as in a mirror the glory of the Lord, are being

transformed into the same image from glory to glory, just as by the Spirit of the Lord." It was a system that, despite its initial grandeur, eventually resulted in spiritual decline and ultimately, spiritual death. Just as stone tablets can't evolve or adapt, the old covenant couldn't bring about lasting and transformative change.

Matthew 6:9-10 (NKJV): "In this manner, therefore, pray: Our Father in heaven, Hallowed be Your name. Your kingdom come. Your will be done on earth as it is in heaven."

Enter, the "new way." With the coming of Christ and the Holy Spirit, a new era emerges. This new way is marked by the life-giving Spirit, who doesn't chisel commandments into stone but writes them on human hearts. The fading glory of the old covenant pales in comparison to the "far greater glory" of the new covenant under the guidance of the Holy Spirit. This illustration highlights the contrast between the external, rigid law of the old way and the dynamic, transformative power of the new way through the Holy Spirit. It encourages readers to expect a more profound and enduring glory under the influence of the Spirit, an intimate and life-giving relationship with Yahweh that brings freedom and transformation rather than condemnation.

If the old way, which brings condemnation, was glorious, how much more glorious is the new way, which makes us right with God! In fact, that first glory was not glorious at all compared with the overwhelming glory of the new way. So, if the old way, which has been replaced, was glorious, how much more glorious is the new, which remains forever! Since this new way gives us such confidence, we can be very bold. We are not like Moses, who put a veil over his face so the people of Israel would not see the glory, even though it would fade away. But the people's minds were hardened, and to this day, whenever the old covenant is being read, the same veil covers their minds so they cannot understand the truth. And this veil can be removed only by believing in Christ. Yes, even today when they read Moses's writings, their hearts are covered with that veil, and they do not understand. But whenever someone turns to the Lord, the veil is taken away. For the Lord is the Spirit, and wherever the Spirit of the Lord is, there is freedom. So, all of us who have had that veil removed can see and reflect the glory of the Lord. And the Lord—who is the Spirit—makes us more and more like Him as we are changed into His glorious image.

"And Jesus cried out again with a loud voice and yielded up His spirit. Then, behold, the veil of the temple was torn in two from top to bottom; and the earth quaked, and the rocks were split." Matthew 27:50-51.

This act symbolised the fulfilment of Jesus' mission—He had borne humanity's sins, vanquished the devil's works, and triumphed over death through His resurrection. This event granted immediate access into the Father's presence for all who turn to Him for salvation.

The greatest obstacle we must overcome is discovering who and what we are in Christ. Paul addresses this matter in his letter to the Corinthians, discussing those of us who have had the veil lifted and now perceive, as in a mirror, the glory of the Lord (2 Corinthians 3:17-18). With the Lord's presence, there is freedom, and with unveiled faces, we behold His glory, being continually transformed into His image.

See also Ephesians 1:3-8

"Blessed be the God and Father of our Lord Jesus Christ, who has blessed us with every spiritual blessing in the heavenly places in Christ, just as He chose us in Him before the foundation of the world, that we should be holy and without blame before Him in love, having predestined us to adoption as sons by Jesus Christ to Himself, according to the good pleasure of His will, to the praise of the glory of His grace, by which He made us accepted in the Beloved. In Him, we have redemption through His blood, the forgiveness of sins, according to the riches of His grace which He made to abound toward us in all wisdom and prudence."

From the instant of our spiritual rebirth, a supernatural event, we became a reflection of our Father. We became vessels for the King of Kings and the Holy Spirit, and carriers of the Father's presence. God desires to involve us in His activities.

When we recite the Lord's Prayer, "Our Father who is in heaven, Hallowed be Your name. Your kingdom come. Your will be done, on earth as it is in heaven" (Matthew 6:9-10 NKJV). We must grasp the profound significance of our words. We are not just uttering a routine prayer; we are requesting the establishment of God's rule on earth and acknowledging our readiness to execute the authority granted to us. We are being called to administer His will here on earth, just as it is in Heaven. This is not merely religiosity; this is about releasing God's power; laying hands on the sick, witnessing their recovery, expelling demons, cleansing lepers, restoring sight to the blind, enabling the lame to walk, and even raising the dead. Does this sound like a lifeless religion to you?

We are called to this; it's what the entire earth has been groaning for. The manifestation of the sons and daughters of God. Individuals who grasp everything God has accomplished through Christ, and walk, believing who they are!

The question that once echoed in the Garden of Eden, "Did God really say?" has morphed into a subtle whisper from the adversary, casting shadows of doubt over our identity as cherished sons and daughters of the Almighty. But as we delve into the teachings of Paul, particularly in the book of Ephesians, we unearth a profound and reassuring truth that dispels the shadows of uncertainty. As believers, we find ourselves lavished with every spiritual blessing that the heavenly realms offer. These blessings are not merely empty rhetoric; they are tangible and divine realities, bestowed upon us by our loving Heavenly Father. Through Christ, we have been adopted into His divine family, destined for a purpose that was eternally designed, and redeemed by the precious blood of our Saviour. We stand forgiven for our transgressions, and the eyes of our understanding have been illuminated to discern the will of God.

This transformative truth fundamentally reshapes our self-perception. From the very moment of our spiritual rebirth, we are liberated from the shackles of sin and uncertainty, free to embrace our authentic identity. We emerge as radiant reflections of our Father's boundless love, carriers of His divine presence, and active co-participants in His redemptive work here on earth. It is through this renewed perspective that we can truly appreciate the profound significance and far-reaching impact of the giftings and callings of the Father, the Holy Spirit, and Jesus, in and on our lives.

These gifts, graciously imparted to us by the Spirit of God, are far from mere tokens of divine favour. They are potent instruments, equipping us to operate effectively within the new paradigm inaugurated by Christ and illuminated by the guiding presence of the Holy Spirit. Each of these gifts serves a unique function, enhancing our capacity to fulfil our God-ordained purpose and bring glory to His name.

With the Holy Spirit working within us, we are enriched by a diverse range of spiritual gifts. These encompass the revelation gifts, which include wisdom, knowledge, and discernment, offering us profound insights into life's intricacies. Then there are the Power gifts—faith, healings, and miracles—bestowing upon us the authority to tap into God's supernatural wisdom and healing capabilities, thus igniting hope, and ushering transformation into a world marked by brokenness and challenges. We are equipped with Utterance gifts, such as prophecy, tongues, and interpretation, enabling us to communicate divine truths and messages. Together, these gifts empower us with divine insight and authority, enabling us to navigate the complexities of life and serve as conduits of God's love and grace to a world in need.

As we wholeheartedly embrace these spiritual gifts and live according to the new way established by Christ and continued through the Holy Spirit, we do so with strong confidence and eager anticipation. Our prayers aren't just words; they are heartfelt requests for God's presence and strength. We fervently ask for His Kingdom to be as evident on Earth as it is in Heaven. As we do this, we are fully aware of our divine authority and the extraordinary privilege we have to release God's life-changing power to impact and transform lives. In this new way, doubts are dispelled, identities are restored, and purposes are fulfilled.

We are no longer haunted by the query, "Did God really say?" Because we have encountered the living God, tasted His love, and received His invaluable gifts. Firmly anchored in the truth that we are cherished sons and daughters of the Most High, joint heirs with Christ, and vessels of His Grace to a world in need, we operate within the parameters of these gifts. As we do so, we emerge as living testimonies of the new way, ambassadors of His love, and agents of His kingdom. In a world full of uncertainty and shadows, we're here to bring some hope and light. With this heavenly light, we walk a path that shows us the way and changes those who search for the truth. We, as vessels of His radiant glory, are witnesses to the enduring power of His Word and the unwavering love that invites everyone to embrace His divine covenant.

Chapter four

KNOWING OUR AUTHORITY

It was one of those magnificent days; not a cloud marred the azure sky, and the gentle sea breeze provided refreshing relief as the four men walked, engrossed in conversation. These men comprised a diverse group, all robust and deeply bronzed by the sun. They had spent over three years closely following the man who now led the way, absorbing His teachings and hanging on every word. They had witnessed remarkable events; the cleansing of lepers, the restoration of sight to the blind, and deaf ears opened, the resurrection of Lazarus from the grave, and the miraculous raising of a young girl who had died. These years had profoundly reshaped their understanding of life.

They followed Jesus up the towering mountain, and as they ascended, something extraordinary occurred before their very eyes. Jesus underwent a transfiguration; His garments radiated with an intense, dazzling whiteness. Out of the blue, two other men appeared, engaging in conversation with Jesus. They recognised one as Elijah and the other as Moses, their identities passed down through generations as revered prophets and judges.

Peter, James, and John, the three disciples, were seized with terror. Peter, in his customary impulsive manner, suggested erecting three tabernacles right there and then. One for Jesus, one for Elijah, and one for Moses. However, as they grappled with the awe-inspiring spectacle, a cloud suddenly enveloped them, and a voice declared, "This is my beloved Son. Listen to Him." (Matthew 17:1 – 13)

The Greek word used for "transfiguration" here is the same word Paul employed in Romans 12:2, urging believers to "be transformed by the renewing of your mind." In 2 Corinthians 3:18, he elaborates on the concept: "And we all, with unveiled face, beholding the glory of the Lord, are being transformed into the same image from one degree of glory to another. For this comes from the Lord who is the Spirit." The word is "metamorphosis," signifying a departure from one's former state to become something entirely new. This transformation process begins the moment we accept Christ as our Saviour and experience rebirth.

So, what does a transformed life look like? For the Christian who is caught in the web of the religious spirit, it is walking into that freedom that Jesus spoke about in John 8:36: "He who the Son sets free is free indeed." It's being suddenly made aware that we have not only been born again in spirit but have been birthed into the great Kingdom of God, where there is freedom to worship, dance, and leap for joy because of all that the Lord has done.

Man did not invent this freedom; it's not how humanity thinks. It was for the joy set before Him that Jesus endured the cross, died, and rose again from the grave three days later, with the keys of hell and death in His hand! He took you and me into His death and His resurrection so that we might become manifested sons of God (Romans 8:12-17).

For those who have not yet met Jesus, it's like a horse that's been ridden all day in a cattle drive. When his owner takes the saddle and bridle off in the yard, the first thing that horse does is go and roll in the sand that's been put there for that purpose. Then, when he is finished rolling, he will stand up and shake all the dust and sand off his body and then have a long drink of water. That horse is free from the burden of the saddle, free from the bit in his mouth, and best of all, he is free from the directions of that man on his back!

Peter's reaction reflected his upbringing under religious teachers. In today's language, it might have been akin to saying, "Let's establish three churches, Jesus—one for You, one for Elijah, and one for Moses—right here on this mountain where this miracle transpired." It's intriguing to contemplate how we would respond under such circumstances!

So, why did the Father intervene? First, to affirm Jesus' true identity, and second, to redirect the disciples' thinking away from religious doctrine toward the teachings of Jesus, centred on the principles and lifestyle of the Kingdom of God: "If the Son makes you free, you will be free indeed" (John 8:36).

While the three disciples beheld the transformation of Jesus firsthand, Paul's teaching emphasised transformation through the renewal of the mind, shifting our thought processes and responses from religious norms to the principles of the Kingdom of God. This transformational process is unequivocally conveyed three times in the New Testament, through both demonstration and instruction.

In his letter to the Romans, Paul, recognising esteemed philosophers among them, emphasised the need to differentiate between worldly and Godly ways. Romans 12:1 opens with a passionate plea for change: "I beseech you, brethren." Paul's heartfelt cry urges believers to offer their bodies as living sacrifices, marked by joy, delight, and willing devotion to God, for everything about God must embody life. Only then can the vital process of renewing the mind begin, liberating them from religious thinking and unfulfilling worship.

Change hinges on recognising the amazing love that our heavenly Father has for us. Once you come to accept that He is a good Father and that there is no turning in Him, you find that your inward thoughts and character will begin to change, and the deceitful schemes of the devil and the entanglements he attempts to weave around believers will be more easily discerned. This is where your sonship becomes manifested, and you begin to walk in an inner authority that you have not experienced before.

Some still cling to the notion that pastors are infallible and must be obeyed unquestioningly, often at the expense of family and personal life. This conformity to worldly standards contradicts the Kingdom of God's ethos. Why did Jesus come to Earth? To confront and defeat the devil's handiwork, unveiling his web of deception in the light of Truth. If we conform to this world, we adopt the likeness of the devil and walk in darkness, just as Jesus told the Pharisees in John 8:44 "You are of your father the devil, and your will is to do your father's desires... he is a liar and the father of lies."

Jesus confronted the Pharisees with a profound revelation, saying, "You are of your father the devil... Whenever he tells a lie, he speaks from his nature, for he is a liar and the father of lies." That's getting in someone's face when you're that blunt!

Let's delve into the Greek of this verse. The phrase "Of your father the devil" uses the Greek word "ek," showing a lineage or origin. It signifies that the Pharisees were the offspring of the devil, in a spiritual sense, inheriting his deceptive nature. The word "diabolos" for "devil" implies one who falsely accuses or slanders, emphasising the deceitful character. Jesus says that when the devil speaks lies, he does so "ek tou idiou," meaning "from his own." This underscores that lying is intrinsic to the devil's nature; he doesn't deviate from it. The term "pater" for "father" signifies the originator or source, reinforcing the idea that the devil is the true source of falsehood.

Now, turning to 1 John 1:7 (NASB): "But if we walk in the light as he himself is in the light, we have fellowship with one another, and the blood of Jesus, his Son, cleanses us from all sin."

We find Jesus emphasising three very important truths:

1. Walking in the light.

2. Fellowship with one another

3. The blood of Jesus.

The phrase "walk in the light" carries a profound Greek distinction. "Peripateo en to photi" can be unpacked further: "peripateo" means more than just walking; it implies living one's life in a certain manner. "En" signifies being immersed or abiding within. "Photi" translates to "light," which represents truth, righteousness, and God's presence. So, "walking in the light" means not just physical movement but living our lives immersed in God's truth and righteousness. It involves aligning our actions, thoughts, and intentions with his ways. It's a call to honesty, transparency, and obedience, all deeply rooted in the Greek understanding of the phrase.

The verse promises that, by abiding in this light, we experience fellowship with one another, which extends beyond mere human connection. It implies a shared spiritual bond among believers who walk in God's truth.

Lastly, the cleansing power of "The blood of Jesus his Son" is an essential Greek insight. The word "katharizo" for "cleanses" signifies not just surface cleaning but a thorough purification, removing all impurity and guilt. It's a continuous action, conveying that as we abide in the light, the blood of Jesus continually purifies us from every sin. The Greek word "katharizo" (καθαρίζω) is where we get the English word "catharsis." In Greek, "katharizo" means "to cleanse" or "to purify." It's about thoroughly cleaning or purifying something, often linked to rituals, or cleansing processes. Now, when we use "catharsis" today, we're talking about a different cleaning; and that is cleaning out our emotions. It's like letting go of strong and bottled-up feelings, especially negative ones like fear, anger, or sadness. We can do this through activities like art, writing, or talking to someone. Spending time in the "secret place" with the Father will help us process and deal with our inner turmoil so that we regain our inner peace and joy.

It is interesting that the Father would connect Fellowship to the cleansing of the blood of Jesus. Now, I know we can go into all the Greek, Hebrew, Aramaic etc looking at the meanings of this scripture, but what God is doing, is underlining for us, that we are one body, the one new man!! And we cannot live successfully without one another in this world. However, after saying all that, there is some amazing and cool stuff the Holy Spirit does for us when we are a yielded sacrifice. The connection between "katharizo" and "catharsis" is about cleaning and purifying, whether it's our emotions, our thoughts, or both. Both ideas involve getting rid of something that's bothering us or holding us back, making us feel better and refreshed.

I encourage you to read accounts of the Mystics of old from the book "Christian Mysticism through History" by Lisa Jo Rudy: the account of "the flying monk", Padre Pio in the second world war in "Padre Pio and America" by Frank Rega: the book "Ladies of Gold" by James Maloney, and "100 Days in the Secret Place" by Gene Edwards. You will be amazed at how much we have lost over the centuries.

Chapter five

REMAINING CONNECTED

During a seminar in Sydney Australia, I experienced something wonderful. The worship began with a song that seemed freshly composed, as I had never heard it before. It centred around the theme of wondrous grace. My thoughts became consumed with what Jesus had done for me, and tears began to well up in my eyes. At that moment, something astonishing occurred—a vision of Jesus standing before me. His presence was tangible, and He looked at me with a smile filled with pure love.

Every single detail was significant to me as to where I was at in myself at that time. You see, what Jesus did for us through the work of the cross was complete! And even now, as I close my eyes and meditate, I can vividly recall His smile. It was a smile of boundless love, joy, and absolute acceptance.

A common pitfall in ministry is losing sight of the wonder and goodness of Yahweh and the needs of others appear to be more important, so we push aside our times of quiet reflection and meditation on His word. The busyness of ministry or the demands of family life can blur our sense of calling because of the demands of worldly systems. Church life can inadvertently transform into a business model, overshadowing the essence of a spiritual family. Performance may replace anointed preaching, and a desire not to offend can overshadow the pursuit of revelation.

As we transition into the prophetic promise of Jesus, which He conveyed to His disciple Peter when Peter had the revelation that Jesus was "The Christ, the Son of the living God," (Matthew 16:16) we can begin to see what we had been blinded to. The church Jesus was referring to is an exhilarating community of people, which includes every believer. Here, we partner with Him from Heaven to Earth, rather than the conventional approach of Earth to Heaven, continuously beseeching the Holy Spirit to come and requesting things from Jesus. Scripture opens a door to a better understanding.

Indeed, there have been remarkable occurrences within the confines of the old system. However, it's crucial to recognise that the old ways are gradually losing their prominence because a Holy Spirit shift has taken place with the dawn of the new. What this signifies is that we find ourselves at a juncture where we must wholeheartedly embrace this fresh and profound understanding of God's Kingdom on Earth.

This "new" isn't simply a change in tradition or practice; it signifies a transformation in our spiritual journey. It calls upon us to grasp God's intentions and purposes to transcend our current human understanding. It's a summons to align ourselves with His divine blueprint, even if it leads us into uncharted territory.

As senior ministers, leaders in the business world, mums and dads entrusted with representing God's Kingdom on Earth, maintaining closeness to the heart of Jesus is paramount. Our words and actions must reflect this commitment.

Through years of pastoring churches, I realise that it's not about numbers; it's about His presence. It's not about theology; it is about revelation, hearing His voice and inviting Holy Spirit to be the senior leader in the context of being deeply connected with God and approaching service, not as mere religiosity but as a joyful expression of love.

In 1972, I attended Faith Bible College in Tauranga, New Zealand, during its early stages. The college was not finished, and we had been asked if we could come early so that I could help with the finishing of the lecture room before the main group of students arrived. The three-month course was really a "Kingdom of God" based course. We were taught the principles of faith and then sent out every weekend to put into practice what we had learned about Yahweh's anointing, power, and ways, and then to step outside of our comfort zone and into the area and realm of faith. This foundation was a most remarkable experience, setting the stage for those who would later venture into missions and ministry. It's amazing to think that seven years later, I would pastor a church in Australia.

Regrettably, about two years later, the "religious spirit" ensnared me. I became enslaved to ministry, available 24/7, rarely taking a day off. And when I did, I was often too exhausted to enjoy it. This eventually led to a collapse resembling a major heart attack in the late 1990s. This marked the beginning of several years of burnout that grew into chronic fatigue.

I share this to awaken anyone heading down a similar path. Foolishly, I used to declare that I would "burn out for God." But the truth is, God doesn't require ask anyone to burn out for Him. We are sons, not slaves. We are covered with His anointing, not our own sweat, and we are learning to enter His rest.

In the context of being deeply connected with God and approaching service as a joyful expression of love, Galatians 2:20 in The Passion Translation says, "My old identity has been co-crucified with Messiah and no longer lives, for the nails of His cross crucified me with Him. And now the essence of this new life is no longer mine, for the Anointed One lives His life through me – we live in union as one! My new life is empowered by the faith of the Son of God who loves me so much that He gave Himself for me and dispenses His life into mine."

Here we see that the Apostle Paul's words highlight a transformative relationship with Christ when He took us into His crucifixion and resurrection.

I Cor. 6:17 (TPT) says "But the one who joins himself to the Lord is mingled into one spirit with Him." This signifies a deep spiritual union: we are now one with Him.

Understanding these and other scriptures about who we are "In Christ", encourage us to live our lives in close communion with

God, serving with love and joy rather than religious obligation. It reminds us that our actions should flow from the deep well of faith, love, and gratitude for the sacrifice made by Christ. This invites a life of service that is motivated by a genuine connection with God, leading to a joyful and purposeful journey of faith.

This is Yahweh's desire for us. Just as Jesus taught His disciples, and now through the Holy Spirit teaches us, we find His desire to include us in His family.

In what is known as the Lord's prayer, when Jesus utters the words, 'Our Father, who art in heaven,' He invites us to approach our Father with the same intimate and familiar connection that he had. It signifies that we are no longer distant from God but have been lovingly adopted into His family. This prayer reflects our status as children of God and heirs to His promises, emphasising the sense of unity and belonging within the spiritual family.

In essence, when we pray using the words of the Lord's Prayer, we are not only communicating with our Father but also affirming our place in His Kingdom, acknowledging the bond we share with Him as His children. Psalm 37:3 urges us to "Trust in the Lord, and do good; dwell in the land, and feed on His faithfulness." The Hebrew word for "dwell," is "shakhan," implying "to settle down, to sit, to abide." This action helps plant roots securely in the soil, preventing movement by external factors.

Isaiah 61:3b further emphasises this idea of being planted, resulting in the glorification of the Lord.: "To give them beauty for ashes, The oil of joy for mourning, The garment of praise for the spirit of heaviness; That they may be called trees of righteousness, The planting of the LORD, that He may be glorified."

By delighting ourselves in the Lord, He promises to plant us. As ministers of the gospel, we will derive great pleasure from the Lord's presence, remaining connected to Him. From this place of intimacy, revelations emerge that transform both us and those we minister to. This enables us to convey the Father's heart to the needy and lost.

During my time at Bible College, my family and I couldn't live on campus as the college was not advanced enough in the property's development to handle families with children. We shared a house with a man I'll call Max. Max had gone through the course ahead of us and was waiting for confirmation of his mission field calling. Anxious and unsure of his preaching ability, Max and I conversed often. One morning, as we talked and prayed, the Holy Spirit showed me a series of visions.

In these visions, I saw Max preaching to a large crowd on a hillside, followed by him being paddled in a canoe up a river. I glimpsed him in four distinct scenarios, all interconnected. Max departed for the airport shortly after, and years went by without news. Recently, I discovered that all but one of those visions had come to pass exactly as I had seen (the outcome of the last vision has not yet been revealed). I cherish the Holy Spirit's movement in these ways, redirecting us and revealing His purposes.

Max returned a changed man, confident in his identity in Christ, having witnessed God's miraculous work through him. This then echoes the timeless invitation of Jesus to His disciples: "Follow Me, and I will make you fishers of men." (Matthew 4:19).

In Matthew 17:20, Jesus presents a challenge: "I assure you, if you have faith as small as a mustard seed, you can say to this mountain, 'Move from here to there,' and it will move. Nothing will be impossible for you." This isn't just your everyday belief; it's a faith that possesses the power to move mountains. It invites us to place our complete trust in the boundless power of almighty God. What's truly exhilarating is that, like the disciples, we too can move in this gift of faith. We can rely on God for the seemingly impossible, not only in our own lives but also in the lives of those we reach out to.

Next, think about the power of the gift of healing. In Acts 3:6, Peter did something incredible when he said, "I have no silver and gold, but what I do have I give to you. In the name of Jesus Christ of Nazareth, rise and walk!" The people were astonished that the disciples could heal the sick. This passage illustrates the power of the gift of the working of miracles. It's not about having some extraordinary personal ability; it's about allowing the Holy Spirit to work through us. We too, can pray for and witness the healing of physical and emotional ailments. And there's more!

As we explored 1 Corinthians 12:4-11, we come across various spiritual gifts, including the working of miracles, the gift of prophecy, and speaking in tongues etc. These gifts are given to empower believers for various ministries, to strengthen the church and demonstrate the power of the Kingdom of God, Christ's rulership on the earth. Now, here's the exciting part: these gifts are not just ancient stories; they are accessible to you today. You can continue Jesus' mission of bringing healing, hope, and transformation to a world that desperately needs it.

It's essential to remember that these gifts are not for personal gain or to show off. Instead, they glorify God and build up the body of Christ.

I want to encourage you. The Holy Spirit can work through you in powerful ways. You have the potential to make a real difference in people's lives. Whether it's through faith, healing, or any other spiritual gift, don't underestimate what God can do through you. Seek these gifts earnestly, and as you step out in faith, you'll grow in your relationship with God and impact the world around you.

As you reflect on these insights, consider your own spiritual journey. Through faith and the power of the Holy Spirit, you can engage in ministry, just like the disciples did. You are called to be a vessel of God's transformative power, bringing hope and healing wherever you go. So, believe in the Holy Spirit's work in you, and let His power flow through you. Our walk with Jesus should be as exhilarating as it was for the disciples. Yahweh remains unchanging, His power unwavering. Everything written about Him is as vibrant and impactful now as it was back then. All His promises stand firm!

Recently, while reading Luke 23, I was struck by the contrast between the two criminals crucified beside Jesus. Only one recognised who Jesus truly was. Both had likely heard about His healing miracles and His ability to raise the dead. One mocked, while the other knew Him. One faced hell, and the other entered Paradise alongside Jesus.

To live in freedom and godly authority, the Holy Spirit reveals truth through Scripture, and every word from Yahweh's mouth. It's our daily sustenance. Without ongoing revelation, we risk becoming religious, arrogant, and controlling.

We see that in Galatians 2:20 the old self has been "crucified" and now Christ's life is in me. This signifies a profound spiritual unity, a shared existence with the Divine.

In essence, it encourages us to live our lives in close communion with God, serving with love and joy rather than religious obligation. It reminds us that our actions should flow from the deep well of faith, love, and gratitude for the sacrifice made by Christ. This invites a life of service that is motivated by a genuine connection with God, leading to a joyful and purposeful journey of faith.

The call of the first disciples, as recorded in Luke's gospel, began with a powerful demonstration of the supernatural interacting with the natural. After a night of unsuccessful fishing, Jesus arrived and told Peter to cast his nets into the deep water. Obedient to Jesus' command, Peter's nets were filled to the point of breaking. This incident revealed the abundance of the Kingdom and Jesus as the door into that abundance where lack is replaced with plenty, and it showed that the Kingdom is available here and now. (John 10 :7)

In Luke's gospel, Jesus taught His disciples to pray for the Father's Kingdom to manifest on Earth and for His will to be done as it is in Heaven. This teaching conveyed that living the Kingdom life is the Father's desire. In John 16:12-15, Jesus spoke about the role of the Holy Spirit, who would guide believers into all truth. The Spirit would reveal things to come and glorify Jesus by taking what belongs to Him and declaring it to us. This shows the supernatural revelation available to us through the Holy Spirit.

While historical revivals and the lives of remarkable individuals inspire, they can't replace the experience of living in the supernatural. Embracing the Holy Spirit's revelation allows transformation from ordinary to extraordinary. For instance, Peter transitioned from Simon the fisherman to "Peter," the rock, upon acknowledging Jesus as the Christ, thanks to supernatural revelation.

As believers, we are both prophetic and supernatural. Living according to worldly values should feel foreign to us.

For who has known the mind of the Lord, that he will instruct Him? But we have the mind of Christ." (1 Corinthians 2:16, NASB)

This scripture highlights our understanding of the intentions and desires of the Lord, which align with Kingdom principles. Our lives should exemplify the wonder of Kingdom living. Kingdom living is showcasing how God lives, in total love, and joy, even to the extent of dancing for joy over us. Heaven is the place where love abounds, pure amazing love! That's our target for this world also, a world where all colours, and races are united in that amazing love.

An Australian school teacher shared an incredible testimony, where he and his wife, along with their four children were missionaries in Tonga. This man had been an accountant, and he could not understand how this could happen, but happen it did! God created money in his wallet while it was still in his pocket!

His accountancy training did NOT allow for this, and he just could not find a "grid" for it!

Instances like these remind us of the supernatural life God wants us to embrace. Miraculous healings further illustrate this life, portraying snapshots of the life God desires for us.

It's disheartening when Christians limit the Great Commission to "preaching the Gospel and making disciples." Jesus' command goes beyond this, as He states in Mark 16:15-18:

And he said to them, "Go into all the world and proclaim the gospel to the whole creation. Whoever believes and is baptised will be saved, but whoever does not believe will be condemned. And these signs will accompany those who believe in my name, they will cast out demons; they will speak in new tongues; they will pick up serpents with their hands; and if they drink any deadly poison, it will not hurt them; they will lay their hands on the sick, and they will recover." This passage highlights the normalcy of the supernatural life Jesus urges us to enter. Embracing this realm doesn't make us "important," or self-centred; rather, it makes us joyfully obedient citizens of God's Kingdom, fulfilling His will right here on earth!

So, how do we stay in connection with the Lord through our busy lives.? There's one proven approach—thirsting for God's presence to envelop and consume us. What we set our heart on; we attract. This entails building a deep relationship with the

Father that transcends surface-level connections. It's a thirst and hunger that only God can satisfy. When God's presence arrives, it's like the gentle breeze that enveloped Elijah in the cave (1 Kings 19:11-13), electrifying every fibre of our being with anticipation. The more time we spend waiting on the Lord in this manner, the more we are transformed into His image, enabling us to naturally flow in the ways of the Kingdom.

In the busyness of our daily lives, it's crucial to remember the essence of staying connected to Yahweh. This connection isn't just an obligation; it's a vital part of our spiritual journey, it's setting our hearts on Him! This is a journey that Jesus encourages us to embrace. It doesn't elevate our status or make us self-centred. Instead, it positions us as obedient citizens in God's Kingdom, actively fulfilling His will.

The key to maintaining this divine connection lies in developing a deep, unquenchable thirst for God's presence. This desire goes beyond casual or superficial interactions; it's a profound longing that only God can satisfy. Just as Elijah experienced God's presence as a gentle whisper, we too, can encounter God in subtle yet profound ways. This encounter is not in the grandiosity of events but in the quiet, consistent seeking of His presence.

By spending time in God's presence, waiting and listening, we gradually transform into His likeness. This transformation allows us to flow naturally in the ways of His Kingdom, making the supernatural a normal part of our lives. Our relationship with God becomes a central part of our existence, influencing our actions, thoughts, and decisions.

Here is a Scripture for Meditation:

"Be still and know that I am God; I will be exalted among the nations, I will be exalted in the earth." - Psalm 46:10 (NIV) This verse reminds us of the value of stillness in God's presence. In our stillness, we acknowledge His sovereignty and power, allowing us to focus solely on Him, despite the chaos of the world.

Chapter six

RECOGNISING OUR AUTHORITY

In the Gospel of Luke, chapter 4:1-2 we find a significant account illustrating the importance of recognising our authority, as demonstrated by Jesus in His confrontation with the devil.

"Jesus, full of the Holy Spirit, returned from the Jordan and was led around by the Spirit in the wilderness for forty days, being tempted by the devil. And He ate nothing during those days, and when they had ended, He became hungry."

Three crucial points emerge from this narrative. First and foremost, it emphasises that Jesus was full of the Holy Spirit. Secondly, Jesus was led by the Holy Spirit and thirdly, Jesus faced temptations from the devil.

In Acts chapter two, the apostle Peter, who had never attended a Bible College but had walked with Jesus for over three years, boldly stood up and delivered a powerful message under the influence of the Holy Spirit. This message led to the salvation of three thousand souls. Peter, a former fisherman, had been transformed by the baptism of the Holy Spirit, and he spoke not from arrogance but from the divine authority of God Himself.

If we desire to walk in true Kingdom authority, we must learn to yield our entire being to the Holy Spirit and understand our identity in Christ. It boils down to this: if we yield, He leads; if we humble ourselves, He imparts His authority to withstand the devil's assaults. Christians are not exempt from the devil's deception and must develop the discernment to distinguish between God's guidance and other influences. The Holy Spirit grants us wisdom and discernment.

When Peter received the revelation of Jesus' true identity (Matt.16:13-16), it marked the beginning of his transformation. Jesus had initially told him, "I will make you fishers of men" (Matt. 4:19). This was Peter's destiny being spoken right out in the open!

It is one thing to be called, and another to walk in revelation. During Jesus's School of Discipleship, Peter and others learned that they possessed authority over demons in Jesus' name and could heal the sick by laying hands on them. They grasped the concept of delegated authority.

However, Peter's denial of Jesus before His crucifixion, serves as a cautionary tale. Neglecting to meditate on the revelations brought by the Holy Spirit can lead to their loss, along with the life they bring. Could Peter have got caught up in the busyness of ministry and lost the life those revelations initially granted him?

Author Ron McGatlin, in "The Basilea Letters," highlights how our limitations, imposed by negative and degrading words, can hinder the full expression of Christ within us.

To break free from spiritual stagnation, we must embrace our authority in Christ, recognising His indwelling presence through the Holy Spirit. Repentance from dead works becomes our first step.

After Peter's denial, his repentance touched Jesus' heart, and he was welcomed back into the fold. From the day of Pentecost onward, Peter and the other disciples operated with an authority and power they had never imagined possible.

Many things can rob individuals of their God-given authority. Elijah, exhausted and emotionally drained after defeating the prophets of Baal, received a threatening message from Jezebel. He fled until exhaustion overcame him, but God intervened, sending an angel to sustain him. Similarly, carrying the weight of ministry alone can cause us to lose our authority, leaving us vulnerable like the burnt stones mocked by Sanballat during Nehemiah's wall rebuilding. (Nehemiah. 4:2 NASB.)

Just as wounded prey attracts predators, the enemy of our souls senses the loss of authority. The restoration process is exemplified in King David's experience when he found his camp raided and his men distraught. 1 Samuel 30:6f says David "strengthened himself in the Lord" and reclaimed what was stolen.

In the Bible, authority and power are intertwined concepts. Authority often represents the right to exercise power. As believers, our authority comes from Christ Himself. In Matthew 28:18, Jesus says, "All authority in heaven and on earth has been given to me." He then commissions us to go and make disciples. This means that as followers of Christ, we operate under His authority. In Acts 1:8, Jesus promises that we will receive power when the Holy Spirit comes upon us. This power empowers us to be witnesses of Christ. It's not a power for personal gain or domination over others but a power to fulfil the mission of sharing the gospel and bringing God's love and kingdom to the world.

The Bible teaches our weaknesses can be opportunities for God's strength to shine through. In 2 Corinthians 12:9-10, Paul speaks of a thorn in his flesh. Three times, he pleaded with the Lord to take it away, but God's response was, "My grace is sufficient for you, for my power is made perfect in weakness." Paul then says, "For when I am weak, then I am strong." This paradoxical truth highlights that in our weakness, we function in Yeshua's strength! Now how good is that!!

Throughout the Gospels, we witness Jesus healing the sick. His healing ministry reveals His compassion and authority over illness. In James 5:14-15, the apostle James encourages believers to call for the elders of the church to pray over the sick, anointing them with oil in the name of the Lord. The prayer of faith will bring healing. It's a demonstration of our authority over sickness and disease.

Scriptures provide principles for managing finances wisely. Proverbs 22:7 warns about the consequences of debt, emphasising the importance of financial stewardship. While it doesn't guarantee wealth, it encourages us to seek financial wisdom and avoid unnecessary financial burdens.

In Psalm 139, we find a beautiful reminder of our worth in God's eyes. Verse 14 says, "I praise you because I am fearfully and wonderfully made; your works are wonderful, I know that full well." Recognising our value and identity in God can help us overcome feelings of inferiority.

The Bible acknowledges the reality of emotional struggles. In Psalm 42, the psalmist expresses deep distress, but he also turns to God for hope and comfort. Learning to hear our Father's voice and believing His promises, are powerful tools for overcoming depression. While the Bible doesn't specifically address medical conditions, it emphasises seeking God's wisdom and guidance in all aspects of life.

James 1:5, we're encouraged to ask God for wisdom, and He will give it generously. Seeking professional medical advice and relying on God's guidance can help individuals manage such conditions. Our authority and power as believers come from Christ, and they are expressed in our dependence on God's strength, our trust in His healing, our financial stewardship, our understanding of our worth in Him, and our reliance on His wisdom in all areas of life.

It's a journey of faith, recognising that through Christ, we can overcome various challenges, not in our strength alone, but in His. It is crucial to remember that our authority extends not over humanity but over all demonic forces, various illnesses, and even death. Jesus entrusted us with a GREAT commission and the power to fulfil it. We inhabit fleshly bodies that require care. Hence, Jesus assured us that He would work through us. In other words, we should never lose sight of the One capable of carrying the burdens we bear.

Matthew 20:1-16 showcases the Lord's grace, generosity, and fairness. Acknowledging these qualities of God as our Father bolsters our confidence and affirms our identity and place within the Kingdom. Hebrews prompts us to mature from infancy, enabling us to realise our true nature. It's unbecoming for an adult to behave childishly, and tragically, such an adult fails to reach their full potential. In Hebrews 5:13, "infant" translates from Greek "νήπιος" (nēpios), denoting spiritual naivety, akin to an infant reliant on milk instead of solid nourishment. Recognising ourselves as born-again sons of God is essential before we can wield the Spirit's powerful gifts and fulfil our destiny. In this critical era, often referred to as the 'last days', the call of the eleventh-hour church is clear: any time is opportune to engage in the Lord's work, with His grace available to everyone.

In Arland Hultgren's New Testament Commentary interpretation of Matthew 20:1-16 we find a parallel of the church, or the eleventh-hour church is exciting. Here we see that the workers hired at the last hour are paid the same as those who toiled all day, underscoring the generosity of the vineyard owner and by extension, the Lord.

[1] "For the kingdom of heaven is like a landowner who went out early in the morning to hire workers for his vineyard. [2] He agreed to pay them a denarius for the day and sent them into his vineyard. [3] About nine in the morning, he went out and saw others standing in the marketplace doing nothing. [4] He told them, 'You also go and work in my vineyard, and I will pay you whatever is right.' So, they went. [5] He went out again about noon and about three in the afternoon and did the same thing. [6] About five in the afternoon, he went out and found still others standing around. He asked them, 'Why have you been standing here all day long doing nothing?' [7] 'Because no one has hired us,' they answered. He said to them, 'You also go and work in my vineyard.' [8] When evening came, the owner of the vineyard said to his foreman, 'Call the workers and pay them their wages,

beginning with the last ones hired and going on to the first.' ⁹ The workers who were hired about five in the afternoon came and each received a denarius. ¹⁰ So when those came who were hired first, they expected to receive more. But each one of them also received a denarius. ¹¹When they received it, they began to grumble against the landowner. ¹² 'These who were hired last worked only one hour,' they said, 'and you have made them equal to us who have borne the burden of the work and the heat of the day.' ¹³ But he answered one of them, 'I am not being unfair to you, friend. Didn't you agree to work for a denarius? ¹⁴ Take your pay and go. I want to give the one who was hired last the same as I gave you. ¹⁵ Don't I have the right to do what I want with my own money? Or are you envious because I am generous?' ¹⁶ So the last will be first, and the first will be last."

The eleventh-hour church is a call to awaken, to recognise that the twilight of opportunity is upon us and that the time for hesitancy is past. It is a rallying cry for the believers to immerse themselves in the urgent work of the 'last days' ministry. How wonderful to see God in the light of his great grace and to know he does not discriminate based on the longevity of one's faith. Rather, he heaps his abundant grace upon every believer who responds to the call, irrespective of the hour.

As we navigate what may well be the final hours of this age, this parable takes on amplified significance. It stands as a rallying cry for believers to actively partake in the 'last days' ministry, reflecting God's continuous invitation to join in His mission, at any and all stages of our lives. It also underlines a poignant truth: "The harvest truly is plenteous, but the labourers are few" (Matthew 9:37, KJV), urging us to embrace our calling with urgency and devotion.

We are presented with a choice in these 'final hours': to actively partake in God's kingdom or to remain idle, under the false security that time is on our side. This decision is key, for, like the workers hired in the eleventh hour, we too are granted the opportunity to be part of the grand harvest, to guide souls to God's kingdom, and to propagate His message of redemption.

Embracing our role as eleventh-hour workers in these last days is empowering. It affirms that our contributions to God's kingdom are valued, no matter our stage in life or faith. It is a time for decisive action, a call to awaken from spiritual lethargy and commit to the task of soul harvesting. Recognising our identity in Christ and our divine calling is essential. As new creations, we are admonished to cast aside our past burdens and woes. "Behold, I will do a new thing; now it shall spring forth; shall ye not know it? I will even make a way in the wilderness, and rivers in the desert" (Isaiah 43:19, KJV). If challenges persist, we are encouraged to seek guidance from the Lord and fellowship with spirit-filled believers. It is time to ascend, as the scripture says, "Arise, shine; for thy light is come, and the glory of the LORD is risen upon thee" (Isaiah 60:1, KJV).

We mirror the anchor runner in a relay race, who strives not only to triumph but to honour those who have preceded him. We are team players, and now is our time to 'turn up the gas' and run this race with fervour and purpose. The verse that speaks of those who went before us is Hebrews 12:1, which says, "Therefore, since we are surrounded by such a great cloud of witnesses, let us throw off everything that hinders and the sin that so easily entangles, and let us run with perseverance the race marked out for us." "The harvest truly is plenteous, but the labourers are few" (Matthew 9:37, KJV).

When we recognise and operate in the authority granted to us through the Holy Spirit, we can resist the enemy's temptations and be empowered for the task ahead.

The Authority Jesus demonstrated in the wilderness is the same authority that empowers us as the eleventh-hour workers. Whether we have been in the faith for a long time or have just begun, the authority we carry as followers of Christ remains the same.

Peter's transformation from a fisherman to a Spirit-empowered apostle who could address thousands is a testament to the potential that lies within each believer when we come to understand the authority we have in Christ. This understanding is not only for those who have been prepared through years of training but also for those who may feel like they have arrived late to the faith.

The Father's love for us undergirds us to move in His authority, that endorses the latecomer in the vineyard, equips them for the work, and emboldens them against the adversary's wiles. The eleventh-hour workers are not just labourers in the vineyard; they are warriors in the spiritual realm, equipped with the full armour of God, ready to stand firm against the devil's schemes and to harvest souls for the Kingdom.

The Father's love empowers us to operate in His authority, affirming and equipping us for His work and fortifying us against the enemy's schemes. As the eleventh-hour workers, we are more than just labourers; we are fearless soldiers in the spiritual domain, clothed in God's complete armour, poised to confront the devil's plans, and gather souls for the Kingdom.

With the Holy Spirit's authority given to each of us, we are called to steadfastly resist temptation, proclaim the gospel with conviction, and live out the entirety of our divine mandate. It is incumbent upon us, irrespective of the timing of our call, to heed this divine prompting, rise with the Spirit's empowerment, and embrace our roles in God's great harvest.

Hebrews 12:2 specifically mentions the joy set before Jesus, which propelled Him through His trials: "Let us fix our eyes on Jesus, the author and perfecter of our faith, who for the joy set before Him endured the cross, scorning its shame, and sat down at the right hand of the throne of God,"

In the Kingdom of God, service is not only a duty but a path to reward. Scripture tells us that God acknowledges every act of service and the sacrifices made in His name. In Matthew 5:12, believers are encouraged with the words, "Rejoice and be glad, because great is your reward in heaven." Similarly, Hebrews 6:10 states, "God is not unjust; He will not forget your work and the love you have shown Him as you have helped His people and continue to help them." From these scriptures, we see that the rewards for service in God's Kingdom are both abundant and eternal.

Chapter seven

EMBRACING DIVINE POWER

As I disembarked at Sydney Airport; the invigorating embrace of the sunlit day greeted me. I had returned to lead weekend meetings at a church I had once pastored. Although this congregation was relatively small, housing nearly a hundred worshippers who loved Jesus, its impact reached far beyond its size. This unassuming church had a global footprint, actively engaged in outreach missions, and the establishment of churches in remote places, including Vanuatu. The current pastor, a fellow Kiwi, and a cherished friend of mine, operated in an evangelistic and apostolic ministry, leading countless individuals into the Kingdom of God.

The evening ahead was their customary Miracle Service, an electrifying occasion to minister in. The worship was transcendental, and after delivering my message, people of all ages congregated with diverse ailments and afflictions, seeking the healing power of God. Conditions like chronic back pain, damaged knees, and debilitating arthritis were miraculously healed. Two gave their hearts to Jesus, while another pair experienced baptism in the Holy Spirit.

Yet, despite these remarkable moments, I sensed something amiss. It had been quite some time since I had last preached, and I felt a void in terms of God's authority and the tangible presence of His anointing.

"Now to Him who is able to do exceedingly abundantly above all that we ask or think, according to the power that works in us." (Ephesians 3:20)

This verse reminds us that God's power within us far surpasses our expectations and prayers. It emphasises that the source of this power is at work within us, enabling us to accomplish beyond what we could imagine.

Returning to the house where I was staying, I went to my room, longing for the Lord's presence. As I began to pray, He began to address certain issues that required my attention in my personal life. This transformed my approach to prayer, and I grew more assertive in confronting oppressive spiritual forces.

Gradually, I felt the restoration of spiritual authority. Hours passed in His presence, and when I got up the next morning, I was restored.

The Sunday service burst forth with a deep presence of God. An hour of spontaneous, free-flowing worship set the tone. My preaching carried a stronger anointing, and I operated in the prophetic, with the authority of God, which released a wonderful healing anointing. All glory and honour belonged to Him alone.

"And with great power the apostles gave witness to the resurrection of the Lord Jesus. And great grace was upon them all." Acts 4:33.

In the early church, the apostles operated with great power as they testified to the resurrection of Jesus. This verse highlights the remarkable grace that rested upon them, enabling them to perform signs and wonders.

The passage referring to the early church and the apostles' powerful testimony to the resurrection of Jesus is of great significance. It not only provides historical insight into the early days of Christianity but also offers valuable lessons on stepping into deeper waters of faith and ministry. In the early church, the apostles played a pivotal role in spreading the message of Jesus' resurrection. Their testimony was not just words but a powerful demonstration of God's grace and resurrection power. This is crucial because it affirmed the central message of Christianity: Jesus conquered death and offered salvation to all who believed in Him. Their testimony served as the foundation of the Christian faith, inspiring countless believers throughout history.

The passage emphasises the "remarkable grace" that rested upon the apostles, enabling them to perform signs and wonders. This grace was not ordinary but supernatural, Heavenly enablement to carry out their mission effectively. It teaches us that as believers, we are recipients of God's grace, which empowers us for ministry and service. It encourages us to rely on God's grace as we step into deeper waters of faith and service, knowing that His grace is more than sufficient for any task.

Just as the apostles operated with great power and testified boldly, this passage teaches us the importance of stepping out in faith. It encourages us to go beyond our comfort zones and embrace the callings and ministries God has placed on our lives. Stepping into deeper waters of faith means being willing to trust God for the miraculous, to proclaim the Gospel boldly, and to rely on His grace to perform signs and wonders in His name.

The apostles' testimony centred on the resurrection of Jesus. This underscores the foundational importance of believing in the resurrection as a core aspect of our faith. It challenges us to deepen our understanding of and faith in this central truth, recognising that it is the source of our hope, redemption, and destiny.

Look for a moment at the life and work of George Müller, a Christian who lived in England during the 19th century. He ran an orphanage and was known for his strong faith and prayer life. His life reminds us of early apostles and their teachings about grace, faith, and the resurrection of Jesus.

Müller's journey started with a big change in his life when he became a Christian. This change was just like what happened to the apostles, and it set the stage for his important work in ministry and caring for others. His life went from not believing in God to being deeply connected to Christian values, showing how powerful the Gospel can be.

One of the most significant things about Müller's work was how much he trusted in God's provision and prayed. He didn't ask people for money, and he didn't get into debt, but he still built and ran several orphanages, helping thousands of orphans. This way of doing things, based on faith and trust in God's guidance, is like how the early apostles relied on God's help and provision.

Müller had some amazing experiences, and he witnessed God directly helping him. These included last-minute answers to his prayers and guidance in tough times. These experiences are authentic examples of living a life of faith and show how powerful God can be, just like in the time of the apostles.

Müller's impact and legacy lasted far beyond his lifetime, just like the influence of the apostles. His way of faith, praying, and serving left a lasting mark on Christian communities and the care of those in need. It shows the strong results of a life dedicated to faith and service.

Müller's life also lines up with apostolic principles in theology. His reliance on God's grace, bold sharing of the Gospel, and living out his faith in action are clear examples of what happens when we trust in God's Word.

In today's terms, the lessons from Müller's faith and service are still really valuable for believers. His life encourages individuals and communities to grow in their faith, trust in God's grace, and be committed to serving others. This is just like what the apostles taught about taking steps of faith and relying on God for the extraordinary.

My testimony from that weekend's ministry experience underscored a vital truth. Drawing near to God in prayer and surrender allows His power to flow through us, enabling us to affect lives and show His love to those we serve. It is in His presence that our authority is revitalised. How outstanding to see His anointing manifest in our ministry! All glory and honour belong to our Heavenly Father. The prophet Ezekiel's vision of the temple and the flowing water in Ezekiel 47 holds profound lessons about stepping into deeper faith, trusting in God's promises, and navigating life's challenges with confidence.

In Ezekiel's vision, he is led to the entrance of the temple where he sees water flowing from under the threshold, symbolising the life-giving flow of God's promises (Ezekiel 47:1). This water also represents God's Word and His divine guidance, which always emanates from His presence.

As we embark on our journey of faith, it often begins with the ankle-deep waters. These shallow waters symbolise our initial steps of faith. We may have heard about God's promises, but we are just beginning to experience them personally. It's like dipping our toes into the water, testing the depths of God's faithfulness. In this stage, we learn the importance of trust—trusting that God's Word is true, that His promises are reliable, and that He is with us in every step we take.

"And when the man went out to the east with the line in his hand, he measured one thousand cubits, and he brought me through the waters; the water came up to my ankles. Again, he measured one thousand and brought me through the waters; the water came up to my knees." Ezekiel 47:3-4.

Do you know God doesn't intend for us to stay in ankle-deep waters? As Ezekiel's guide measures off a thousand cubits, the water gradually deepens. It reaches knee-deep, and then it rises to the waist. This progression reflects the stages of growth in our faith. We trust God more deeply, and as we do; we wade into waters that challenge us. In knee-deep waters, we may face trials and obstacles that test our faith. We learn to lean on God's promises and rely on His strength. It's in these moments that our confidence in Him deepens, and we discover God is true to

His Word. Just as the water rises to our waist, we realise that God's faithfulness can sustain us even in difficult circumstances.

Then comes a significant turning point—a river that is too deep to cross, waters deep enough to swim in.

"Again, he measured one thousand, and it was a river that I could not cross; for the water was too deep, water in which one must swim, a river that could not be crossed." v5

This represents a mature, unwavering faith that fully trusts in God's promises. We recognise that God's Word is not merely a shallow stream, but a mighty river that can carry us through life's challenges. In these deep waters, we experience the fullness of God's presence and His transformative power.

As Ezekiel is asked, "Do you see this?"

"He said to me, 'Son of man, have you seen this?' Then he brought me and returned me to the bank of the river." v6.

We, too, are prompted to reflect on our faith journey. Have we grown in our trust in God's promises? Have we ventured deeper into the river of His presence, where we can swim in the depths of His love and grace?

In Ezekiel's vision, the river flows eastward into the Arabah, bringing life and freshness wherever it goes.

"Then he said to me: "This water flows toward the eastern region, goes down into the valley, and enters the sea. When it reaches the sea, its waters are healed. 9 And it shall be that every living thing that moves, wherever the rivers go, will live. There will be a very great multitude of fish because these waters go there; for they will be healed, and everything will live wherever the river goes." v 8-9

Similarly, as we step into the deep waters of faith, we become conduits of God's blessings to others. Our lives overflow with His love, and we affect those around us with the living water of His Word.

May Ezekiel's vision inspire us to trust in God's promises, to venture into deeper faith, and to become vessels through which His life-giving river flows, bringing hope and transformation to a world in need

.

Chapter eight

ANCHORING OUR FAITH

In our journey of faith, it is essential to focus on two specific aspects and maintain consistency. It's crucial to walk confidently with God and avoid becoming what some might call a "loose cannon." This term originated from the days of sailing ships, particularly during the age of naval warfare, describing a cannon that fired either 12 or 18 pounds of metal in the shape of a ball. If one of these cannons came loose during a storm, it would roll around the deck, causing significant damage and potentially even going through the bulkhead into the sea. Sailors, in their attempt to secure these 'loose cannons', could end up being maimed with a crushed leg or foot, especially when an unpredictable, violent wave struck the side of the ship.

Over time, the term "loose cannon" developed to be used metaphorically, describing individuals or situations where someone's actions or behaviour are unpredictable, disruptive, and potentially harmful because they have become a law unto themselves. It implies a lack of control and the potential for disastrous consequences, much like a heavy cannon rolling uncontrollably on a ship's deck.

Identity and destiny are the two important realms of understanding that we must pay attention to, and therefore any prophetic words that have been spoken over you need to be gone through prayerfully and with attention to the details after the excitement and wow of the moment has left you.

Both Annette and I have received numerous prophetic words spoken over us. (Ha-ha, I must admit, my dear wife is the one who types them out; my typing is more of a 'hunt and peck' style!). We have been very diligent about re-reading them and praying about the promises, decrees, and direction that they have brought to us. One particular prophet who we greatly respect has prophesied over us three times over an eight-year period. We are amazed at the way they have linked up over the years, underlining and confirming that which the Lord had led us into or spoken about to us.

I share this to encourage you to get your prophetic words out and blow the dust off them and prayerfully go over them again, underlining the parts that are truly ringing your bell, so that you can keep praying over them, and your diligence catches the attention of the Holy Spirit, leading to further understanding and affirmation within your spirit.

Turning our attention once more to the subject of identity, we find a profound revelation in the Scriptures, specifically in Romans 8:14-16 as conveyed in The Passion Translation. This passage delves into the essence of who we are as individuals and our relationship with the Divine. It illuminates the concept that true maturity as children of God is not measured by religious obligations or the paralysing fear of never measuring up. Instead, it unveils a remarkable truth, the presence of the "Spirit of Full Acceptance". This divine Presence is like a warm embrace, that draws us into the family of God, assuring us we will never experience the anguish of feeling orphaned or abandoned. As this divine presence stirs within us, our spirits harmonise with it, resounding with tender affection, addressing God as "Beloved Father." The Holy Spirit, like a gentle whisper, makes God's role as a loving parent tangibly real, echoing deep within our innermost being the loving affirmation that we are, indeed, God's beloved children.

Once we firmly establish this truth within our spirit, fear and anxiety find no foothold, and they simply slip away from us, akin to water sliding off a duck's back as it peacefully rests and floats on the surface of a lake or river, safe in its natural habitat.

Identity leads us towards our destiny. It has been said that our scrolls, containing our destinies, were written out before the world was even formed, and we were manifested onto this earth as squalling little bundles of wrinkled flesh that brought so much joy to our parents. This is about a loving Father at work, creating all that we see and wonder at. Ephesians Chapter 1:4-5 say this: "Just as He chose us in Him before the foundation of the world, that we should be holy and without blame before Him in love, having predestined us to adoption as sons by Jesus Christ to Himself, according to the good pleasure of His will, to the praise of the glory of His grace, by which He made us accepted in the Beloved." This is a SELAH moment, a time to stop and think upon it, to meditate, chew it over and over in your heart until it becomes revelation truth within you!

These are the foundational truths upon which your destiny will flourish or flounder! For Jesus, the revelation that Peter had of Him being the Christ, the Son of the living God, was the foundational truth upon which Jesus said He would build His church.

Dear reader, God gave us such a beautiful gift through the Holy Spirit when He gave us the ability to "see" in the spirit (revelation) an important truth suddenly becoming revealed to you in a way that changes you in your spirit man.

We need to see and understand that this is what Jesus said to the devil when he was tempting Him in the wilderness to change stones into bread. Jesus said in Matthew 4:4 "Man shall not live by bread alone, but by every word that proceeds from the mouth of God." Our heavenly Father is the source of all good things, and we have His DNA!

Now, another aspect rarely spoken of in connection with the believer's destiny is our becoming "one spirit" with Christ. This can be found in Galatians 2:20, 1 Corinthians 6:17, Acts 17:28, and 1 John 4:17b in The Passion Translation of the Bible.

So, let's delve into these amazing scriptures that truly bring our identity and destiny closer together. First, we have

Galatians 2:20: "My old identity has been co-crucified with Christ and no longer lives. And now the essence of this new life is no longer mine, for the Anointed One lives his life through me—we live in union as one! My new life is empowered by the faith of the Son of God, who loves me so much that he gave himself for me, dispensing his life into mine".

This revelation should deeply affect all of us who believe. Have you realised the incredible significance of this? Jesus Christ, the Saviour of the world, the One now seated at the right hand of the Father, the King of Kings, and Lord of Lords, has infused His life into our lives, making us one with Him! Wow, wow, wow!

Then, we have 1 Corinthians 6:17, which says: "But the one who joins himself to the Lord is mingled into one spirit with Him." This can be illustrated by pouring two glasses of water into one glass and they mingle together and can never be separated again! Can you see the glorious linkup with the scripture above? But that's not all, for Acts 17:28 tells us: "It is through Him we live and function and have our identity; just as your poets have said, 'Our lineage comes from Him'."

This is why we need to understand who we are and where we are going as individuals. This is where genuine prophetic words spoken over you should be brought before the Lord so that you receive the fullness of His message and can begin to walk in the areas, He has called you to.

Remember that a prophetic word spoken over you should confirm what the Holy Spirit has already spoken to you, providing comfort, confirmation, or edification.

I love the testimony of King David's journey from a shepherd boy to a king. The notable thing in this story is the working of the power of the anointing that came upon him when the prophet Samuel poured out the anointing oil upon him amid his brothers (that would have caused quite a stir!). The Spirit of the Lord came mightily upon David from that time. He even killed a lion and a bear that was attacking his father's sheep with a sling and a shepherd's crook! A little while later, he faced something even bigger, a giant named Goliath. David went out to face him, took a stone out of his pocket (Hehe, I couldn't resist that one!), and slung it at the giant, killing him. Then he cut off Goliath's head with his huge sword! All of this came from the power of the anointing that was on his young life!

When the Holy Spirit comes and touches your life, you will never be the same. Nothing but following the calling on your life will satisfy you. Mothers, if you love spending time with your children and being able to continually speak into their lives, that is a great calling! Never belittle it, for you are helping to shape future generations!

A turning point in my early Christian years came in the early hours of one morning when I was awakened by the Lord Himself, calling me into what proved to be an apostolic/prophetic calling. In the years that followed, this calling took my late wife, Yvonne, our three children, and myself into a life of the miraculous and into the restoration of broken churches. It was a joy to see those churches healed and bringing forth fruit that attracted growth. I can truly say that my God is a wonderful, loving, and altogether good Father!

The need for fathers in the day that we live in is very great. However, for some reason, great-hearted men seem to be shy of filling that place of need. Sure, it's not the high-profile ministry that some have, but don't forget that it is not the man who is giving you this ministry, but the Father Himself. That's why He gives you an understanding of His heart for His children. Being that kind of father is not about being there all the time; it's more like being there for someone if and when they need to hear words of wisdom and encouragement. We don't live their lives for them, but we cheer them on from the sidelines.

As I near the end of this book, I'd like to share my thoughts on a much-written topic: "Hearing God's voice." This is something that we can make too hard for ourselves, leading to frustration and giving up. Alternatively, we can step into it as easily as putting on our shoes.

The simple fact is that God is always speaking. All we need to do is learn to listen with an attitude of believing expectation.

Here are two simple steps to follow. Firstly, believe that Father thinks highly of you and loves you so much that He wants to chat with you and share exciting things. Secondly, stop pleading with Him and try sitting quietly with your Bible, "Watching to see what the Lord would say to you." (Hab 2:1) Please notice that Habakkuk says both "Look" and "Hear", and he does this from a state of alertness, but also from a place of rest.

Meditate on the image of Enoch walking with God in close communion and let's contemplate the deep enrichment of Enoch's heart during these moments. Enoch's connection with God was so deep that something truly extraordinary occurred: God extended an invitation for Enoch to remain in His presence, and Enoch was no longer found on Earth because God had taken him. This remarkable testimony is a wellspring of inspiration, igniting a deep yearning within me for a similarly profound connection with God in my own life.

In the Book of Genesis, it's recorded that Enoch lived for 365 years before God took him. The text describes Enoch as someone who "Walked with God," signifying a close and loving relationship with Him, and then simply vanished, as God took him (Gen 5:21–24). Enoch's life and journey stand as a powerful testimony of a godly individual whose walk and life were pleasing to Almighty God.

So, my reader, hearing and seeing in the spirit realm is not so difficult, because we are in Christ and are seated with Him in heavenly places from the time, we came to Him and became born again in our spirit. We became a new creation, and new means new! Old things have passed away, and new things have come. Some of those new things include being able to live your life as a "dead person" (Galatians 2:20).

Now, that's pretty neat, don't you think? If you have been having trouble with your past haunting you, this scripture is your ticket out of jail. You now know that you have total authority over every lie of the devil and can speak to it with absolute confidence. Why? Because it is no longer you that lives, but Christ lives His life through you! His authority is also your authority. Why? Because you are one spirit with Him, that's why! (1 Corinthians 6:17) Thank you, Jesus.

One of the most difficult things for most people is getting past what religion has taught us from our very first church visit. We must transition out of that way of thinking into the way that Jesus opened up for us, which was freedom from every restriction that had blocked us in the past. Romans 12:2 talks to us about this situation and tells us to: "Stop imitating the ideals and opinions of the culture around you but be inwardly transformed by the Holy Spirit through a total reformation of how you think. This will empower you to discern God's will as you live a beautiful life, satisfying and perfect in His eyes". (The Passion Translation)

Did you ever consider yourself to be worthy of His love and His sacrifice? Did you ever really realise that the work of the cross was "a complete and amazing thing" and that it was done for us? The bible is the most amazing and exciting book in the world, it's full of adventure, and nail-biting edge-of-the-seat, moments if we read it that way. He was the One whose heart was crying out for a family that He could pour His love upon and out of that desire came the greatest story ever told!!

Parents, please make the bible an exciting book when you read it to your young children and teach them how to use their imagination to bring it to life.

As I am now at the end of this writing, my prayer is that something written on these pages will catch your attention enough for you to pause and think about it, and that out of those thoughts will come a life-changing revelation.

A Suggested Prayer for you.

Yahweh, in life's ceaseless demands, help me find stillness in Your presence. Cultivate within me a deep thirst for You, a desire that surpasses all earthly distractions. May Your gentle whisper guide me through each day, transforming me into a true reflection of Your love and grace. Amen.

www.ingramcontent.com/pod-product-compliance
Lightning Source LLC
Chambersburg PA
CBHW051451290426
44109CB00016B/1705